Praise for

Text Messages to My Sons

"A must-read for anyone seeking to raise empathic and connected teens and adult kids."
—MARCY AXELROD,
TEDx Speaker and bestselling author of *How We Choose to Show Up*

"Tammy J Cohen has hit it out of the park with this roadmap for creating and sustaining the deep and meaningful connection every parent longs to have with their teenage or adult children. More than just another how-to, *Text Messages To My Sons* taps the world's greatest thinkers and cultural icons to help you communicate your deepest values to your kids—and deliver your message right to the palm of their hand! Divorced or alienated parents will find a great ally in this warmhearted strategy of consistent, one-way missives of love and support."
—TRACY POIZNER,
Strategic Consultant, Un-Deletable Dad

"*Text Messages To My Sons* is powerful and groundbreaking! As a stepmother, it took me a while to understand that connecting today requires another communication mode. Tammy's book sheds new light on how I can connect and reach without preaching. Thank you!"
—JANE UBELL-MEYER,
founder of Bedside Reading

"An inspiring read that aims to motivate parents to go beyond simple texts and offer their kids encouragement, valuable lessons, and boundless love."
—CASEY SKEEN,
Casey Reads

"*Text Messages to My Sons* transcends traditional parenting advice by bridging the communication gap between parents and children. This gap is often brief or lost in the noise of our daily lives. In a world dominated by social media and devices, where our voices can feel muted, this book provides a meaningful way to reconnect with our children.

After reading it, we were so moved that we immediately shared it with our grown daughters and sons, encouraging them to pass it along to their peers. Tammy Cohen's heartfelt texts offer a clear road map for reconnecting with our children and grandchildren, creating more profound, more meaningful bonds.

This book is a treasure and should be shared widely, especially with young parents navigating the chaos of today's world. More than just a parenting guide, *Text Messages to My Sons* is a touching and motivating reminder of the importance of genuine connection in an age of disconnection. It's a powerful testament to the lasting impact of simple, thoughtful communication.

—MONICA STOLLER and LINDA PRETTER,

co-hosts Chasing Fabulous TV

"Tammy J Cohen has a deep passion for sharing light, love, and support with others and encourages readers to do the same. Parents can learn how to communicate with their children and children with their parents.

As a former caregiver, I appreciate text messages and highly recommend sending messages to caregivers to show support as well.

I have interviewed Tammy J Cohen twice on my radio show, *Chatting with Betsy*, and I know her passion and authenticity shine through. Thank you to Tammy J Cohen for writing this highly recommended and inspiring book; it is a beautiful gift any time of the year!

—BETSY WURZEL,

host of Chatting with Betsy on Passionate World Talk Radio Network

"As soon as I heard about this book, I was hooked! *Text Messages to My Sons* offers a unique approach to bridge the communication gap between parents and children in the digital age. Through a collection of thoughtful text messages that Tammy sent to her sons, she demonstrates how to convey love, wisdom, and support using a familiar format. Her concept blends timeless wisdom with modern technology, providing parents with a practical tool to strengthen bonds and impart valuable life lessons. Inspirational and accessible, it serves as a guide for fostering deeper connections in an increasingly disconnected world. Tammy, thank you for sharing your wisdom and how we can communicate with our kids in a chaotic world."

—TONYA EBERHART & MICHAEL CARR,
founders of Brand Face and Hosts of Be Bold Branding Podcast

"As a parent coach and advocate for over 30 years, I've seen firsthand how challenging it can be to maintain communication and connection with our kids as they grow older. That's why Tammy Cohen's *Text Messages to My Sons* resonated profoundly with me. Tammy masterfully captures the essence of modern parenting, where simple, heartfelt texts serve as lifelines for connection—even when there's no response on the other end.

What I loved most about this book is Tammy's unwavering commitment to showing up for her kids, even in the most minor ways. She sends these texts without expecting anything, proving that it's not always about what we get back on but about letting our kids know we're here for them, no matter what. This collection of messages reminds all parents that we don't have to have the perfect words or wait for the ideal moment to reach out. Sometimes, just showing up on their phone is enough.

In her expanded edition, Tammy doesn't just share more of her journey; she also equips parents with practical tools and suggestions for how we can adapt these messages to fit our unique relationships with our kids. In a time where technology can often feel like a barrier between parents and teens, Tammy uses it as a bridge, offering us a way to connect on their terms.

With her signature humor, honesty, and warmth, Tammy reminds us of the importance of keeping communication lines open, even when complex. Whether navigating the teenage years or trying to stay connected with a young adult, *Text Messages to My Sons* is a powerful reminder that connection isn't about getting it perfect, it's about showing up repeatedly.

—JACI FINNEMAN,
founder of No Problem Parenting and
Host of the No Problem Parenting™ Podcast

"*Text Messages To My Sons* is a powerful reminder to parents that we alone are responsible for teaching our children how to give and receive love and support through communication—a step-by-step guide to fostering the most profound family relationships.

—RUDI RIEKSTINS,
Top 5 Coach, speaker, host of The In Powered Life Podcast
Anniston Riekstins, author of *The Universe Is Hiring*

Text Messages to My Sons

A Guide to Using Mobile Devices to Connect and Communicate with Your Kids

Tammy J Cohen

broad
book
press

Broad Book Press, Publisher

Interior book design by Claudine Mansour Design www.claudinemansour.com
Photography by Gail Hadani www.gailhadani.com

Paperback ISBN: 9781963549188
eBook ISBN: 9781963549195

Published in the United States by Broad Book Press, an imprint of Broad Book Group, Edwardsville, IL.

Library of Congress Control Number: 2025903631

To David, Aaron, and Joshua

*You inspire me to be a better person and to continue to evolve.
You are the greatest blessing in my life.*

To Sidney

*Thank you for being my life partner, for your love,
and for sharing this journey with me.*

Contents

Foreword

by David, Aaron, and Joshua Cohen

When our mother told us she was writing a book about her daily morning messages, we thought, *What an amazing idea!* There is more than enough content for five books from those messages, but even 100 books of messages would not be enough because the value of a loving, thoughtful message from a mother to her son is infinite. As cliché as that may sound, and as unappreciated as our mom may feel when we don't give a lengthy response or we just "love" the message, knowing we have a mother who loves us enough to send messages every day and cares enough to put thoughtful, motivational, and wise insights into every message has a deep and lasting impact. It is one that almost gives us an unconscious belief in ourselves and our value that can't be shaken by external forces and doubts.

There are times when our mother's messages are exactly what we need to be told, where it's almost as if G-d is speaking to us through her. There are times when the messages may seem too long or we don't get to them until later in the day, but we've always found those messages are especially meaningful and give insights that strengthen our resolve. They have shown us the power of motivation, positive thinking, and intentions. They provide motivation on days when we most need it. Sometimes they contain useful tips and facts we'd probably never know if we didn't have a mother who is always learning, evolving, and sharing her wisdom with us. It's been a privilege to receive these messages, without fail, day in and day out, and now that gift will be given to the entire world.

Mom, we are so proud you took the leap and made this book. You always reinforce our beliefs in ourselves, and now we want to use this foreword to reinforce our belief in you! We can't wait to see a day when parents all over the world will be sending their children loving, insightful, impactful, and meaningful messages every day.

Introduction

Technology has changed our lives, so I embraced it, but mostly, I tried my best to keep up. It started with email, and then I figured out texting on my flip phone. The first thing I did was text my kids, who were a lot younger at the time. It just seemed really easy to send a message, as I knew they would at least look at it. Plus, as a parent, reminding your kids feels like nagging, so sending a message is a good memory jogger of what you want them to do.

Typically, the texts were reminders, requests, or questions, and to be honest, their texts to me were basically about what they needed or wanted done, like:

- "I will pick you up at . . ."

- "What do you want for . . ."

- "Where are you . . ."

- "Pick this up . . ."

- "I forgot this or that: Can you bring it . . ."

- "I need money for (fill in the blank) . . ."

- "Can I have or do . . ."

The truth is, as the kids got older, my texts began to take on my verbal communication style of nagging, scolding, or giving unsolicited advice. I would often send these long texts, speaking and writing out each word one-handed (I never mastered the two-handed thumb texting), and I would actually proofread before sending. I usually sent them while angry, exasperated, fed up, or on autopilot.

And my sons would usually either not respond at all or just give me a one-word response, like a "Ya," a "No," or some acronym with which I was totally unfamiliar. Sometimes we got into it, and I always felt bad afterward.

For those of you who have sons, daughters, or any kids with whom you communicate regularly, there is a stage where they just don't want to converse or have discussions with anyone except their friends or whomever they deem as cool or worthy. There is no exact length of time for this stage; it really is an individual thing.

In addition, I was usually working or traveling for work, so the texts to my kids were mostly logistical and purposeful, to structure or organize their time and my time to get things done and make sure everyone was safe and where they were supposed to be. I never even thought about communicating with them in a different way. It was just about telling them what to do or going through a checklist of some sort.

It wasn't until the pandemic, when everything stopped and I was no longer traveling constantly, that I started to think about my life and existence. I remember thinking about where I was mentally, physically, spiritually, and emotionally, and I realized I needed a big reboot. It was also at the same time that my sons had moved out or were moving to the next stage of life. I really started thinking about my relationship with them. What patterns had I been repeating for years, and did I do and say the wrong things?

We don't realize growing up how much of our family dysfunction and origin story sits with us and forms who we are. As advanced as we think we are, our minds are ancient, and in many ways, we accept everything we see around us from a young age. We subconsciously learn at a young age to fit in with the tribe we are born into. We learn and inherit a lot of stuff, good and bad, and we pass this on to our progeny and so on.

When everything shut down at the beginning of the pandemic, I had the time to take stock of myself. I realized I was not happy and needed to figure things out. Suddenly, there was all this time to go inside and look into my mindset, and I did not like what I saw. So, I began to immerse myself in programs, coursework, and seminars, learning how the mind is wired and works. I was learning about the effects of thoughts and beliefs. I was learning about how much of what we believe comes into being at a young age. It was a very enlightening time for me. I was reading books written by visionaries and leaders, and I thought I would love to share this knowledge and wisdom with my kids.

I was unsure about how to go about it; after all, my sons are grown, and even if they were all living at home, the truth is that most young people are not that interested in having in-person conversations. But everyone is invested in their phones. Everyone seems to have their phones completely accessible in hand, in their back pocket, or a bag. People are super engaged with their devices and living for the pings and distractions. It is rare to see people having a conversation at a restaurant; most of the time, they are looking at their phones.

According to research, the average person checks their phone every 12 minutes, roughly 80–100 times per day, and for Gen Z Americans, it amounts to about 7 hours a day.

Texting is not new. When my sons were growing up, I texted them either reminders, commands, or reprimands. This was the context for the majority of the texts that I sent them daily. When I thought about how I communicated with them, I decided that while immersed in my personal development, growth, and spiritual journey, I would change the conversation entirely with my kids. I wanted to evolve and change how I interacted with my sons. I longed to be someone they wanted to hear from. I also realized that to communicate, I would have to use the same technology that is distracting and engaging be-cause, as noted, devices are the most accessible form of communica-tion today, and I knew my kids would look at their phone messages.

I began in January of 2021, sending text messages to my sons and sharing the wisdom I was learning. I was not lecturing but shar-ing. The messages became heart-centered in a short time because I naturally included my love for them, gratitude, inspiration, and the wisdom I was sharing. I learned that love and gratitude are the highest-frequency vibrating energies. I knew I wanted to direct this energy to my kids, and every time I hit "send," the fantastic, beautiful energy affected me, too.

As I continued to work on my development, I became accountable to my kids in my messages. I shared my mistakes and shortcomings, apologized for all the times I yelled, said, and did mean things, and wanted them to know it was never about them; it was me and my triggers and negative reactions.

You must model it if you want your kids to respect, love, and connect with you. If you want your kids to be accountable, you must be responsible and own your stuff. This is not to say you need to be best friends with your kids but be in tune.

The most remarkable part of this journey was the transformation in my relationship with my sons. As I continued to send daily messages, they began to see me as a human being, with my own set of challenges and struggles. They showed me compassion, understood my journey, and were proud of me for moving forward. This shift in our relationship was a testament to the power of consistent, heartfelt communication.

I NEVER SET OUT TO WRITE A BOOK

Honestly, it never occurred to me to publish one at all. I just wanted to send these beautiful messages to my kids. I had to build a habit and realized this is not a one-and-done, love-you-honey thing but a daily commitment. Over time, I would tell a friend or colleague about my daily practice, and they would comment, "Wow, that is fantastic. You should write a book." So, I did.

Text Messages to My Sons: Connecting Deeply in a World of Devices debuted on October 4, 2023, and the response was overwhelming. I received moving messages from readers who found the book profoundly resonating and inspiring. It was as if a light had been switched on, and they realized that they too could use text messaging to express love, inspiration, gratitude, accountability, and share wisdom. The book provided a starting point for those unsure of what to message, and they could then personalize their messages from there. The unexpected positive outcomes of my daily messaging journey inspired others to try.

It wasn't until October 7, 2023, that I fully grasped the importance of my mission on this planet. I saw the pervasive hate, violence, misinformation, indoctrination, and propaganda that constantly bombard our kids and us through social media platforms and digital channels. This realization underscored the importance of my mission to counteract these negative influences and foster positive, meaningful connections.

A study by the Pew Research Center in 2023 highlighted that 62 percent of young adults aged 18–29 have encountered misinformation on social media platforms, often without the skills to distinguish between credible and false information. This exposure can create issues such as anxiety, depression, and disconnection.

In addition, research indicates that many young people in the U.S. feel disconnected from their parents. According to a survey by Springtide Research Institute, about 40 percent of young adults aged 13–25 report feeling lonely and disconnected from their parents and other adults. This sentiment of disconnection can negatively impact their mental health and well-being, contributing to feelings of loneliness and isolation. Furthermore, a 2023 Institute of Family Studies report found that around 35 percent of young adults aged 18–29 feel a lack of strong emotional bonds with their parents.

There is a ton of research on the topic of disconnection, and as parents, we intuitively know there is an issue. We know that we need to make the effort to engage in communication with our kids to build stronger relationships that increase connection and weaken feelings of disconnection.

So, the question is: What we can do in a society that does not foster connection, even though there are more ways to connect today than in history?

The answer is simple. Reach out to your kids wherever they are and use whatever works with no expectations. People are on their phones and devices continuously; this is a fact, so message them there, where they will pay attention and see it. Kids are not interested in having an in-person conversation for the most part, and if they happen to be present for one, they may be checked out while you are talking.

The key is having no expectations for a response back. You take it upon yourself to message love, to let your kids know how worthy they are, how incredible they are, and how blessed you feel to be their parent. You send that high-frequency energy their way, and not only will you get the energy hit when you send it, but they will receive the energy hit when they read it. Imagine how much high frequency; beautiful energy would be out there if everyone sent and read these kinds of messages daily.

My kids often do not respond to my messages, and they are not the "Mommy, I love you" type, but I know what it means to them that there is a person in their lives who cares enough to reach out daily. I have spoken with parents who are upset that their kids don't respond and say that they are not going to keep messaging. My advice to them is, do not stop; this is not a conditional thing; love is unconditional. You do it to strengthen your connection to your kids—not necessarily to expect reciprocity. Because this will matter to them even if they act like it does not. I do not know anyone at any age or stage who does not want to know that their parents loved them and thought highly of them.

These beautiful messages have had a tremendous effect on my relationship with my sons. It has mattered to them to the extent that they wrote the foreword to the book, and I hope you have taken the time to read it.

After readers' incredible responses to my first book, I realized that it was just the beginning and that I could produce a more expansive work based on feedback I received over the past year from industry experts and my audience. I want to take everything I have learned since self-publishing and improve on it. The book you hold in your hands (or in your e-reader) is the result.

I realized that I sent messages about learning, growing, improving, trying, taking chances, and failing and that I had to apply this wisdom

to myself. I even asked my future self if I should go for it and produce this expanded edition. My future-self answered, "Absolutely."
My mission is to start a movement to get parents and individuals to
message love, inspiration, gratitude, accountability, and share wisdom daily.

To that end, this book represents the way I evolved as a parent to
use technology to connect on a deeper level with my sons. In it, I give
examples of text messages that any parent or person can send or just
incorporate and make their own. As you read, keep in mind that these
messages are organized by topic, not in a linear order. I have tried to
retain my "texting style" in these examples, which means you may see
use of acronyms, numerals in lieu of spelled-out numbers, shortened
phrases, and truncated sentences. And, like any other parent, I revisit topics and concepts over time when I'm trying to drive a message
home with my kids. My intent is not to tell anyone how to communicate with their children or promise that what has worked for me will
do the same for you, but rather to show you what worked for this parent and perhaps inspire you to start rethinking how you text with your
own kids. I do hope you enjoy reading the texts as much as I enjoyed
writing them. My big hope is that you will build connections in your
own way by sending text messages of love, inspiration, and knowledge to your loved ones. Find your words and emojis; speak from your
heart.

I hope anyone reading this book will be inspired to explore new
ways of communicating and connecting with their loved ones,
whether they are children, siblings, extended family, spouses, or
friends. The impact is undeniable.

This powerful gift lies within each of us. We need to share it one
message at a time.

CHAPTER 1

Gratitude Appreciation

One of the reasons I started messaging my kids daily was to share what I was learning. During the pandemic, I had time to look at myself, and I realized I was not okay. One of the first principles that I immersed myself in was feeling gratitude. I spent many years feeling like a victim or not worthy. Everything changed when I started understanding the importance of being simply grateful for life, my sons, a roof over my head, food, family, friendship, income, etc. I changed because feeling gratitude and appreciation brought more positivity into my life, which in turn promoted a state of well-being. I started to see opportunities instead of limitations. I began to see the positive traits in others and build stronger relationships. My emotional resilience grew, and I believe my mental health improved. I knew I could not expect my kids to be grateful or appreciate anything if I could not consistently practice it in my messaging and acts. I wanted them to experience the joy of gratitude, to feel uplifted and inspired by the simple things in life.

Good morning ☼**, and here we go!** The most important thing to remember is that another day is a gift. Being present is a present. When you look at each day this way, you are filled with promise, gratitude, and happiness. Add in the notion of how loved, respected, and truly wonderful you are, then understand it's the recipe for a magnificent day. Even if a roadblock comes up, you have the capacity to easily handle it because you start each day knowing the above and are grateful for having the opportunity to open your eyes and greet a new day. Sending you bazillions of blessings and my love ♡🖤🤍 every minute of every day!

Good morning ☼**!** I hope you're staying warm during this freeze. Here is a follow-up on my message from yesterday about letting emotions like frustration, anger, or impatience take over in a situation or turning a situation into an apoplectic occurrence. I ran across this interesting quote from **George Orwell**:

> *"The energy that actually shapes the world springs from emotions."*

So, think about what a world this would be like if people were healthy emotionally. Think about the energy we would feel regularly if emotions were positive. We cannot change the world, but we can start with ourselves. If you can just take a moment to stop negative emotions by taking a few deep breaths and asking, "Does this serve me?" What if we just replaced an angry thought with an amusing one? Any one of these will break a negative cycle.

Once the anger dissipates, the left and right sides of your brain will start communicating, and your energy will change immediately.

Those around you will subtly pick up the shift to positive energy, and things will be better. Doing this 1x monthly, weekly, or daily will make all the difference! No one said it is easy to do but give it a try. I love ♡🖤🤍 you so much! Have a blessed and positive energy day!

Good morning ☼**!** Hurtling toward another weekend! Today, the sun is out. Make the most of a beautiful day. Take a moment to walk and remember to breathe deeply. Breathing is the most essential of all things. Breathing is more essential than water or food. Breathing helps the mind to rest. This is particularly apparent when you are focusing deeply to create, solve a problem, or achieve something. The brain can only focus intensely for up to 1 ½ hours. It is imperative to rest your brain, which is easy to do because all it takes is taking a few minutes to walk and BREATHE. Remember, your brain is running many other functions, too, so adding deep focus, which is what we go into when we are really into a project, takes a lot of brain energy. Give yourself the break needed so your brain can recover.

Where do you think the term 'sleep on it' came from? It came from those who work on something into the morning hours. The truth is the mind is no longer functioning optimally, so pulling all-nighters is not all that effective. Usually, if you sleep on it, you have new and fresh thoughts in the morning that supplant what you had previously come up with during an all-nighter. You have an incredible mind, which I love ♡♥🩶, so remember to nurture and protect it.

Good morning ☼! I hope you had a lovely and restorative weekend! I still can't believe we are heading into the last month of the year. It is fitting that the first night of Hannukah leads into the last month of the lunar calendar. But as children of the moon calendar, remember to always be the light. Always lead and be ready to help. Listen to other people and try to understand versus cutting off, making fun of, or disparaging. There is nothing glorious or cool about humiliation; it just shows insecurity from the person doing the humiliating. Light is only seen by those who open their eyes. This is why the menorah remained lit, so the Jewish people could see with clarity what was right and true. May light always shine in your path, and may you be a source of light unto the nations. I love ♡♥🩶 you and believe in you.

Here are some techniques to protect your energy and emotions:

1. Imagine white or blue light covering you and forming a protective field over you from the person.

2. Become the observer and remove yourself from the situation. And see what is really going on with the person trying to hurt you.

3. Put yourself in a mindset of love and calm, so that is what you feel.

4. Imagine something funny, like the person who is upsetting you is blowing up like a balloon and floating away with air coming out of their ass. You will laugh, and that breaks the effects of unhappiness.

5. Think of my love ♡♥🖤 for you, and I hope that will make you smile too.

Good morning ☼. Even though I woke up later than usual, and as always, my first thought was you! I'm not surprised about this because I'm the luckiest person to be a mom to the most extraordinary kids in the world. I managed this three times. Now that's a WOW! After thinking about you and how lucky I am, I prayed and blessed you. No matter what time I get up, that's part of my routine. Sending you an infinite and endless amount of love ♡♥🖤 and blessings, always and forever.

Good morning ☼! As we enter the weekend, I was thinking about how great we would all feel mentally and physically and how wonderful the world would be if we just saw the good and the beauty in everything. I will always see this in you. I love ♡♥🖤 you.

Good morning to my ☼ **miracle!** I give thanks for your existence! I bless you continuously. Be happy with yourself and who you are. Be confident in your ability and believe in yourself. Don't measure yourself against anyone else; the only measure you should do is with yourself. There is nothing you cannot achieve, but a good place to start is by achieving happiness and inner peace first, and this comes from feeling grateful. I love ♡♥🖤 and adore you.

> *"Remember, being happy doesn't mean you have*
> *it all. It simply means you're thankful for all you have."*
> **—Unknown**

Good morning ☼! I am looking at my plants, staring out the window, thinking how lucky I am to live in a nice place with space, have a roof over my head, a bed to sleep in, protection against the elements, heat in the winter, cool air in the summer, food to eat, a coffee maker, a gym, a rooftop. As human beings, we really do not need a lot. What we do need is to remember to appreciate whatever we have and be kind. To show up as a leader, not a victim, a visionary, not a follower, a creator, not a copier. Remember, the truly big people are the ones who make others feel bigger. We have a duty to be considerate of others. Quaker **Étienne de Grellet** stated it this way:

> *"I shall pass this way but once; any good that I can do*
> *or any kindness I can show to any human being, let me do*
> *it now. Let me not defer nor neglect it, for I shall not pass*
> *this way again."*

As I look out this window, I think about you and how much I love ♡🖤🤍 and adore you.

Good morning ☼**!** The weather is changing. *"Winter is coming."* I put some *Game of Thrones* in there! But really, winter is not a bad thing. It's a season. Back in the day when starvation and lack of heat was a real thing, well, winter sucked. But as I look forward, not backward, and I hope you do too, a change of season is a good thing and part of the rhythm of life as G-d created it. Enjoy the crisp fresh air, the beautiful colors of leaves changing, and the approach of my favorite holidays, Thanksgiving and Hannukah. I love ♡🖤🤍 you from the depths of my soul every minute, every day.

Good morning ☼**!** Another Friday, and as we move into the holiday season, I think it's especially meaningful to start with a holiday that is all about gratitude and recognizing how lucky we are. When thinking of gratitude and positivity, I realize it comes down to shifting your thoughts from negative to positive.

Here is a concept called *CTFAR* from **The Life Coach School:**

- *C. Circumstances:* Something happens, which in reality is a neutral event.

- *T. Thoughts:* You assign a thought to it based upon your beliefs or experience.

- *F. Feelings:* After you have this thought, then come feelings associated by the thought.

- *A. Actions:* You act based on the feeling that was generated by the thought.

- *R. Results:* What is the result of this thought, feeling, or action? Did it cause an outcome? Is it showing itself physically?

The logic is that every event is neutral. Our beliefs interpret or give meaning to these events. A negative thought will produce a negative feeling, action, and result, which can lead to terrible energy, attracting more terrible energy and defeatism, as well as physical malady. Positive beliefs or the removal of limiting beliefs brings positive thoughts. Positive thoughts bring feelings that produce high frequency, powerful and uplifting energy, and produce amazing results.

The same can be said for gratitude. Assign the thought of gratitude. I am grateful for this event because it taught me something, or because it showed me a better way, etc. See how your thoughts about any event in your life matter. Be the observer of events before assigning thoughts to them. Remember, they are neutral and not about you.

When you think or have a thought, ask yourself, "Is this thought serving me? Or is this feeling serving me?" Do not even allow yourself to stay in a negative thought or blow up a neutral event in your mind. I love ♡🖤🤍 you madly—beyond comprehension.

Good morning ☼! I love you to the moon and back. You make each day a joyful one for me. G-d is with you every step of the way, and so am I.

grat·i·tude

/ˈɡradəˌt(y)ood/

noun

the quality of being thankful; readiness to show appreciation for and to return kindness.

This is what I feel for having you in my life. I am grateful to have sons like you.

Good afternoon ☼! It's still morning here in Dallas as I am heading to Utah for the WBTT Retreat. I was thinking this morning about Mother's Day yesterday. I was thinking how lucky I am to be a mom.

Moms give so much but get so much in return. For lucky moms, love is way higher than grief. Thank you for making me a lucky mom! Thank you for making my day really special. I loved it, and I love ♡🖤🤍 you.

Good afternoon ☼! Most people think of Thanksgiving as a day to stuff yourself—no pun intended (stuffing is a Thanksgiving staple food)—and watch football, but it is way more than that. It is a time to connect with family and be grateful for all you have. When I was at the wedding last night and catching up with everyone, I realized that all that glitters and sparkles is just upon the surface. You think someone's life is great because they look really good. You check out everything they have on and build a whole story in your head about how lucky they are and how amazing their life is. At the wedding, a dear friend of mine said: *"You just don't know what is really going on in someone's life or world. You just do not know the truth."*

I already came to this conclusion a while ago and was happy she did, too. But I know at the end of it all, you must be grateful for the things you have. Be very grateful you are happy, you are loved, you are not alone, you are healthy, and you can pay your bills and always have income. But mostly, you are at peace with yourself. These things are what most people wish for.

I love you ♡🖤🤍 and have a wonderful day!

Good morning ☼! I saw this and said, "YES—brilliant!" According to **Napoleon Hill,** values, character, and ethics play a big part in becoming rich, along with a growth mindset. You are a person with a high moral fiber, great character, solid ethics, and values. Don't ever lose these. Love ♡🖤🤍 you forever!

Good morning ☼! I hope this morning finds you happy and full of optimism. I hope you wake up with gratitude. It's the best way to start the day. When you wake up thankful as your first thought, you will be immeasurably happier. The first thing I think about in the morning after my prayers is asking G-d to bless you, and then I add my blessings.

Remember, you are a luxury ship, not meant to sit in a harbor day in and out but to go out to sea. Yes, the sea may get rough, choppy, and challenging, and some days are flat while others are glorious, yet you stay the course, always moving forward toward your destination. I love ♡🖤🩶 that about you.

Good morning ☼ to another glorious day. Every day is glorious when you wake up! It's so simple that we take it for granted. It is such a miracle and blessing to wake up daily in a bed, in a nice place, healthy, with our bodies functioning correctly, food available to eat, a job, purpose to our day, and the knowledge that we are loved. This is a real gift. Don't take it for granted, and may you know you are loved ♡🖤🩶 and blessed deeply always.

Good afternoon ☼! What a warm day! Another late October humid one—except no AC! In NYC buildings, it is a thing to turn off AC, etc., by a certain date. We totally get spoiled about conveniences. I often wonder what people did back in the day without AC, internet, cell phones, tech, etc. They were probably very happy and less stressed out!

Gratitude is something we should always practice; being alive is a gift, and every day you get to learn, grow, achieve, exist, and stay healthy is a blessing! Marry the blessings with simplicity and awareness of conveniences, but not dependent or distracted by them, and life will always be sweet.

You're my blessing. I love ♡🖤🩶 you so much. It's really that simple.

Good morning ☼! Another gorgeous day! I have been thinking about the concept of kindness. I think this time of year brings out this type of thinking more than perhaps any time of year but just think how this world would flip in a minute if everyone practiced kindness regularly. I just read a quote by **Maya Angelou**, which is probably what triggered me to write this today. She said:

"I've learned that people will forget what you said, people will forget what you did, but people will never forget how you made them feel."

That is so deep. Basically, build people up, don't tear people down. Help people who need it, and if you have nothing good to say about someone or something, just don't say anything. Treat people with dignity, kindness, and respect. I'm going to really start living this.

I think the world of you. My love ♡♥🖤 for you is endless.

Good morning ☼! We had our monthly Women Beyond the Table call this morning, and now I am going to a client's office, followed by a wedding in Long Island. It was a bit of a long day, but I am going to approach it all with a smile. You do know that a smile is an upside-down frown. It takes more muscles to frown, believe it or not, than to smile. Since smiling is easier on the face than frowning, you would think more people would naturally do it. Think about the impact on society and beyond if people just smiled most of the time and were more kind.

I think when you smile, not only do you look more beautiful, but you also make life more beautiful. You make my life beautiful every day, and I love ♡♥🖤 you, my beautiful son!

Good morning ☼! I hope your weekend was relaxing and nice. I was driving upstate with Aunt Biggie. I was thinking I have had the pleasure and experience of moving my kids, whether it was to summer camp, college, overseas, new apartments, etc. Always helping them go to the next experience and stage of life. It's quite an honor for me to do this. I used to feel it was a bit of a chore, tiring, and expensive, but now I realize how lucky I was to have been part of these experiences with each of you.

First, I have gratitude to be part of a new year or the end of a year of accomplishment.

Second, I got to create a special memory with each of you that was multi-layered—humor, exasperation, and pride!

Third, I got to watch you stand on your feet and create a second home, your own space, that you would be responsible for and live in.

Fourth, I got to meet your friends, old and new, and see how you have always surrounded yourself with great friends.

Even when issues and challenges came up, you managed to navigate well and come out on top. You will always find a way to rise to the top, even when you don't think so or it looks tough; I know you will.

Thank you for having the guts to leave home and go out there and give me these experiences and memories that will stay with me forever. I will always be available to help you in whatever that next stage is or whatever you need, and thank you for letting me!

Sending you great love ♡🖤🤍 and appreciation.

"He that walketh with wise men shall be wise." —Unknown

Good morning ☼! I hope you had a beautiful weekend and enjoyed it. I was lucky enough to attend my 40th, actually 41st, high school reunion. A true milestone for me! It was phenomenal. I really had an amazing time and realized how fortunate I am for the simple fact to be alive, seeing people from my youth, and revisiting friendships. We were all so grateful to have the opportunity to be together again. The saying _"youth is wasted on the young"_ is so true because as you age, you realize so many things—what's really important and what is not. People are people, and you have more in common than less. That's my insight for the day! I send you love ♡🖤🤍 and blessings. Have a great one!

Good morning ☼! Can you believe it's Friday again? Didn't I just write that I can't believe it's Friday a few days ago? I am spending time thinking about what's important. I was walking around yesterday in Wynwood Walls, Miami, and saw a sign on the sidewalk that said:

"Do you love yourself?" Another art sign said: "Smile." I saw messages about kindness everywhere and about treating people nicely. I said to myself, _there are no coincidences—these messages are meant for me._ Then I read this quote last night from **Henry James:**

"Three things in human life are important. The first is to be kind. The second is to be kind. And the third is to be kind."

No coincidence this quote found its way to me. I said it's easier to smile than frown; it's easier to be nice than mean. I send you skyscrapers full of love ♡🖤🤍 and blessings always!

Good morning ☼! I was thinking about how we take things for granted, like waking up in the morning, that everything is going to be fine, and you are just going to wake up, and it's all good.

Today, people in Ukraine and in Russia, along with many people in the world, don't know what to expect when they wake up. Many people don't even wake up. It takes many synchronized bodily functions to even just allow you to breathe and open your eyes in the morning.

Praise and thank G-d, take care of yourself as best you can, and have gratitude that you don't live in a war-torn land and that there is stability.

I have gratitude for you. I love ♡🖤🦷 you with every fiber of my being. I pray for safety and for peace.

Good morning ☼ **another great weather day.** Live in the moment and take advantage of the weather. Go outside and walk—just breathe and enjoy the air. Not the usual NYC purposeful walking or with thoughts occupying your time. Just enjoy the moment. I have been learning about energy and many of its aspects. I am quite convinced it is a very important and powerful state to harness at the highest level. Energy vibrates at certain frequencies, and the higher the level, the more positive the energy you give. I am sending extraordinarily high frequencies of love ♡🖤🦷.

Happy Rosh Hashanah! I send you blessings and love every day; I don't need a New Year date to do this. I also am refraining from wishing you a sweet year because we all know sugar is the enemy. But I am praying really hard today for good health and fitness because without it—everything else becomes that much tougher to achieve. May the energy of this year, a year to break out and achieve greater heights, flow into you and through you. May we all be inscribed in the Book of Life to continue to love ♡🖤🦷, bless, and share in each other's lives. May it be beautiful and joyous.

Good morning ☼! Another beautiful day. I really appreciate these days; summer is winding down to fall, which has its own beauty and rhythm before the starkness and purity of winter. I saw this today and thought *how simple, how true*. It's about giving and being of service. **Tony Robbins** said:

"Be a blessing to others, and your life will be blessed beyond measure."

I know I'm blessed to have had you!
Know you are deeply loved ♡🖤🤍, valued, and blessed always.

Good morning ☼! The environment is an extension of your mind. Enlightenment is when you know what you know. The field is limitless. A flower blooming in a storm is stronger than a tree blooming under a rainbow. You are my flower always blooming and my strongly rooted and tall tree. I really am lucky to have this, an incredible son, who brings out the desire to achieve and be a better version of myself.

So, thank you from the bottom of my heart, which loves ♡🖤🤍 you endlessly.

Good afternoon ☼! As long as we wake up, finish the day in peace, go to sleep and wake up the next day healthy, it's a WIN and I'll take it each and every day with gratitude. What matters to me most is your health and happiness. Everything else is just icing on the life cake. And at the end of the day the good stuff is right in front of us and around us if we want to partake in it. ♡🖤🤍

Good afternoon ☼! I hope you're having a good day and enjoying the balmy February weather. The two best emotions are love and gratitude. They are emotions that fall into the elevated category whereas anger, fear, frustration, and defeat fall into the limited category. Elevated emotions will regulate gene function so you have good health. Fear, scarcity, judgment, hate, survival, and stress turn off the genes responsible for good health. It's our choice. Love is the highest vibrating frequency energy, and I think it's good to remind people to feel love and express it. I think it's better to do this every day. So that is why I send you boundless love ♡🖤🤍 daily plus a double dose today.

Good morning ☼! I hope you are enjoying the long weekend. I'm mixing work with pleasure today, however I do enjoy work so it's a pleasure, too.

I guess that's the point—to enjoy what you do so that it's less work and more pleasure. Even when work has challenges, it's more of a "learning something new" challenge than an "I can't do this anymore" challenge.

Since people spend the majority of their hours at work, you would think that more people would work in a field or business that they love or enjoy. But this is far from the case. So, I feel blessed that you are in a position to work in something you love or enjoy and are in a field you want to be in. It's definitely something to be grateful for. I love ♡🖤🤍 who you are and what you do.

Good morning ☼! Another Friday! As we hear news about another crazy or dark thing happening in the world, it's easy to say, "WTF?" But then if you take a moment to say, "I am fortunate; the lucky one," then everything falls into perspective.

Greek philosopher **Epicurus** commented on desire and contentment: ***"Do not spoil what you have by desiring what you have not; remember that what you now have was once among the things you only hoped for."*** You are what I hoped for, and I love you for who you were, are, and will be. We can conjure a beautiful memory anytime. We can give love freely with no conditions attached, and we can smile which takes less muscles to make happen than frowning does. It's the simple things that are the best.

You are the best thing to happen to me and this love ♡🖤🤍 is the greatest.

Good morning ☼! We are energy traveling faster than the speed of light. We move and flow with G-d's universe. If you tap into this high-level energy and are open to it, great things happen because the universe wants to give to you. According to **Dr. Joe Dispenza**, ***"When you change your thoughts you change your life, when you change your energy, you change your state of being."***

You can create whatever you want. It's not dependent on external happenings; it's an internal job.

I am grateful that I live in a time and universe where I have you as my son. I love ♡🖤🤍 you with every fiber of my being.

Good morning ☼! When I was younger, I loved Friday because it was a night to go out and party. Well so was Thursday, Saturday, and any other night, but you get my point.

Now, I'm home on Fridays, but I get to slow down and see my three favorite people. It brings me great happiness and pleasure to listen to your conversations, watch you eat, plus take food home too! Having you at the table brings me warmth. My soul feels that it is different from the rest of the week, and I'm grateful for it. I love you ♡♥🖤 very much and appreciate it that you make the effort to be home for Friday night dinner.

Good morning ☼! When I think of my life until this day and every day after, please know that you are everything that is good and perfect in my life. G-d knew this and brought you to me. You bring me peace, joy, gratitude and pride. Because of you, I know what love ♡♥🖤 is and I feel it. This is what my birthday means to me.

Good morning ☼! The last Friday before August! I cannot believe we are already midway through the 3rd quarter of 2023. Here is my message for the day: Beautiful souls recognize beautiful souls. Keep being genuine, be you, and your people will find you. You are beautiful inside and out, and I am in awe that I gave birth to you and raised you. I love ♡♥🖤 you and everything about you.

Good morning ☼! I hope your day is starting off with gratitude and a great outlook plus high frequency energy! If your days start this way you can manifest anything!

I saw this quote and had to share it. As a hard-working person who is dedicated to their career and craft, I thought you would get a kick out of this:

> *"Opportunity is missed by most people because it is dressed in overalls and looks like work."* **—Thomas Edison**

As a Gen X/ Baby Boomer, I think it applies to Gen Z, but Edison lived a long time ago so it may have been as relevant in the past as it is now. You,

I am proud to say, see opportunity and are not afraid to go for it and put the work and effort in! It's one of the many things that I love ♡🖤🩶 most about you!

Good morning ☼. What a cold morning. But like everything else it will pass and then we will complain about the heat. I think the simplest messages are often the best, like this one:

> *"Always pray to have eyes that see the best in people.*
> *A heart that forgives the worst, a mind that forgets the*
> *bad and a soul that never loses faith in G-d."*—Unknown

These are super powers to me. I will spend the rest of my life striving for this. I will always see the best in you and always forgive you. I guess the work is in doing these things for others. The work is in becoming empathetic. I especially want to learn to forget the bad. You are my anchor to be better in this life. ♡🖤🩶

Good morning ☼! I am prone to celebrate love every day and don't need a holiday to recognize it. However, I am happy that there are days in the sun and moon calendars dedicated to the concept of love. Energy wise, love has the highest frequency on the planet. Gratitude is number two. So, let's celebrate love whenever we can because it's about producing the highest level of positive life energy to protect us from the soul-sucking, hate-producing tech algorithms that we are being programmed into.

> *"Where there is love, there is life."* —Mahatma Gandhi

You are my love ♡🖤🩶 and my life.

Reflection: BEING THANKFUL IS A BLESSING

As I reflect on this journey of gratitude and appreciation, I see how profoundly it has shaped my life and the lives of those around me, especially my sons. What began as a personal shift during uncertainty became something more significant: a legacy of positivity and connection.

Gratitude didn't just change my outlook; it changed my relationships. By focusing on what was good and abundant rather than what felt lacking or overwhelming, I discovered the power of perspective. The beauty of gratitude lies in its simplicity and finding joy in life's small, ordinary gifts. When I embraced it, my sons began to feel it, too.

The messages I sent, born from this place of thankfulness, weren't just words. They became reminders to pause, to notice, to celebrate. They became connection threads, weaving us closer even when life pulled us in different directions. Gratitude taught me that you can never run out of things to be thankful for as long as your heart remains open to receiving them.

To my sons, I hope you always carry this practice with you. Life will throw its share of challenges your way, but gratitude will be your anchor. It will remind you of the steady, unshakable blessings in your life.

Let gratitude become your guide. Teach it, share it, and live it, not only for your own well-being but also to inspire those you love. Gratitude is more than a practice; it's a way of being.

CHAPTER 2

Accountability Mindfulness

We expect our kids to grow up and be accountable and mindful; we believe that part of adulthood is being responsible and conscious of others. Just because this is a rational line of thought does not mean your kid will be accountable or mindful of others. They have to see it in action. I struggled to be accountable because I lived in the blame and resentment game for years. I regularly got triggered and reacted. I found it easy to blame others for my situation. I found myself sending messages trying to explain my behavior at times. I wanted them to know that my actions and shortcomings, like yelling, screaming, and saying and doing hurtful things, were not because they had done anything wrong. It was not them; it was me and my issues. I had to take responsibility and be accountable and mindful to them. Practicing accountability and mindfulness fosters independence and teaches us to take responsibility for our actions to become more reliant and strengthen our character. I wanted my sons to know I could learn from my mistakes and make better decisions. Being mindful helped me to reduce anxiety, stress, and reactive behavior, plus have a calmer approach to difficult situations, which my sons noticed. Once you send these types of messages, they go deep. My sons started to see me as a human being, and my accountability had an empowering impact, making them feel more in control of their actions and decisions.

● ● ●

Good morning ☼! I was thinking about how to protect our feelings, so we are not hurt by others. People can be thoughtless in what they say or think. People can put others down and not be supportive of loved ones or friends. Some say it comes from jealousy, insecurities, inner stress, or their own low self-worth, but nonetheless, their words hurt and make for unhappiness. I know I have been that person who may have caused you unhappiness over my reactions, things I said, or mean comments I made. I regret these actions deeply.

    I never meant to be that person but was lost in my own unhappiness, unworthiness, frustration, and despair, which I took out on you. I hope you know I never meant to be that short-tempered, irritable, impatient person. ♡🖤🩶

Good morning ☼! First, I need to apologize for not realizing it is National Son's Day. I honestly celebrate you every day as you are a true star in my life; however, I will do my best to celebrate this day on social media going forward! I personally find these morning messages more meaningful than a yearly SM post! I love ♡🖤🩶 you and do not need a holiday to tell you how awesome you are!

Good morning ☼! A sunny day is always a pleasure to wake up to. I was thinking about the last 2 years and how much I have evolved and become more confident. I feel this happened because I invested in my personal growth and professional presence and capabilities. To attain growth and capability, I sought out coaches, education programs, courses, webinars, conferences, books, and networking opportunities. Education is the vaccine against disruption and stagnation. The leader who keeps learning keeps leading. Learn to love who you are becoming. The day that I stop learning and think I know everything is the day I lose. As you know more, you do better.

"Education is the kindling of a flame, not the filling of a vessel." —Socrates

"Wisdom is not a product of schooling, but of the lifelong attempt to acquire it." —Albert Einstein

Knowledge, when applied the right way, is power.
I love ♡🖤🩶 you and the way your brain learns and works!

Good morning ☼! Lovely day and another week until the end of another month! Thought before the weekend—no matter what part of life you're in 20s 30s, 40s, and so on, you need to keep growing and take stock of what you are doing and where you are at. Even if you are at the proverbial top of your personal and professional life and everything is a win, you need to evaluate and continue to evolve, grow, and change. It takes a great amount of accountability and self-awareness to do this. To be able to check in regularly with yourself. To change what is not working and to maintain and grow what is. It's the inner work that has the greatest impact and drives the external choices. Take it from me, as I am coming to terms with this later in life.

Remember:

"What you are not changing, you are choosing."
—Unknown

I choose to send you messages! I love ♡🖤🩶 you!

Good morning ☼! Here we go into another weekend and closer to Yom Kippur atonement. I think it's brilliant we have the time each year to seriously reflect and contemplate mistakes we have made and things we not only need to apologize and ask for forgiveness for but to also be accountable for.

Be self-aware. I think we learn the most from mistakes and wrongdoing if we allow ourselves to. But the only way to really learn and allow us to is by owning it.

We also must accept that we made a mistake. No excuses, no blaming others. Then reflect on the why and then how to do things better going forward.

This, I think, is what Mechila is about. It's about us making things right between ourselves and others and between ourselves and G-d. Forgive me if I have upset you (I'm sure I have) or said something that hurt you (I know I have). Know it pains me to ever hurt you, and I must work on keeping my emotions from getting the best of me at times.

Sending you love ♡♥♥ always.

Good morning ☼! I am thinking about you, which is not unusual for me. I really like sharing things I find meaningful or profound. I wish I had someone who did this for me at any point in my life. I started to do it for myself not long ago.

My mornings growing up were filled with anxiety and trauma on some days, and my young adult life had a lot of self-doubt and seeking external validation.

This phase lasted a while! But you are the vast improvement to my life, and that is all I could ever wish for. Be strong in your belief about how worthy and amazing you are.

> *"Wouldn't it be powerful if you fell in love with yourself so deeply that you would do just about anything if you knew it would make you happy? This is precisely how much life loves you and wants you to nurture yourself. The deeper you love yourself, the more the universe will affirm your worth. Then you can enjoy a lifelong love affair that brings you the richest fulfillment from inside out."* **—Alan Cohen**

Do you think Alan Cohen is related to us? This is precisely how much I love ♡♥♥ you from the inside out.

Good morning ☼! I'm back! I really missed sending these messages of love to you, but the compensation was having you in person during vacation. I loved knowing I would see you regularly and enjoy the sun, warmth, nature, beauty, and meals together. I love doing mom things for you, too. What was best was feeling so proud of you and the adult you have become. I never thought much about family vacations because when you were little, they were a lot of work, lots to pack, plan for, and make happen. Just flying on a plane with all 3 of you was a challenge! What I realize now is those were the best times. I regret passing on our family vacations for work over the years. I realize letting any time go that can be spent with you and choosing to do something else is a mistake. Let's make a promise to always find the time to take a family vacation and build beautiful memories in the sun and warmth and celebrate each other and the beauty around us. This is what life is about. I have gratitude for the opportunity and love ♡🖤🤍 being your mother.

What is my advice for this year?

> *"When you can't control what's happening, challenge yourself to control how you respond to what's happening. That's where your power is." —Unknown*

Good morning ☼! I really enjoyed spending the weekend together. It has been a while since we spent 3 days together. It was a while ago when we all lived together all the time, and I must say I miss those times and wish I had been more present and engaged instead of waiting for the school week to start. I felt overwhelmed and tired often, and frustrated, and it affected my time with you. I apologize for that, and it weighs on me. I should have been more present, patient, and loving. I wish I knew then what I know now.

I love ♡🖤🤍 you tremendously and always have. It might not have always seemed this way, but it is the truth.

Good morning ☼! Birthdays are a wonderful thing. To watch you grow, change, and learn from year to year. Watch you achieve and accomplish small things and big things. Watch you deal with challenges and figure out a strategy to deal with those challenges. Watch you make plans, have dreams, and see you succeed.

For me, the celebration and gratitude of the birth of each one of you was and is the defining moment of my life. I'm not a person who gives love easily; I did not feel it growing up, so it truly amazes me how much love and gratitude I have for each of you. I try daily to express it, but there are no words big enough to express it. Just know that you are the greatest; truly extraordinary, you are a masterpiece. I loved ♡🖤🤍 you in my past lives, present life, and will for eternity.

Good afternoon ☼! Can you believe it's another Monday? I keep marveling over and going back to the passage of time. Then I saw this proverb and thought about time. Time is a gift, and what we do with it counts. Are we productive? Are we fulfilled?

Are we progressing to a goal? Are we serving? Are we leading? Are we happy? Or are we just busy for the sake of being busy (I get into this sometimes)? Or are we wasting time (another thing that I need to work on)? Don't be a time waster!

> *"There are hundreds of paths up the mountain, all leading to the same place, so it doesn't matter which path you take. The only person wasting time is the one who runs around the mountain, telling everyone that his or her path is wrong."* —**Hindu Proverb**

The most productive time for me is when I tell you I love ♡♥♥ you and bless you.

Good morning ☼. This past weekend was a good experience because I learned more about what I need to improve on. I'm great at conversation, connecting and big picture thinking. Selling, however, is not my strong suit. This was evident at the conference. It was challenging for me to push book sales and close or to walk up to someone and sell.

I felt unsure and out of step. So, I realized this is something I need to work on and have confidence.

I realized that there is always an opportunity to grow and develop new skills, that regardless of age you are never at a point where you know if all. If you get to the point where you think you know it all, you will probably get stuck. So, it is time for me to step out of my comfort zone and move forward.

> *"Life is like a bicycle. To keep your balance, you must keep moving."* —**Albert Einstein**

Balance and movement are good things. You are my balance in this world. ♡♥♥

Good morning ☼! I have the good fortune of being part of a PQ program founded by Shirzad Chamine. It is quite brilliant.

PQ stands for Positive Intelligence Quotient and measures the percentage of time your mind is operating in a calm, executive-thinking mode driven by positive emotions like empathy, creativity, and curiosity.

All too often we are also subjected to negative and self-sabotaging emotions. These are at the subconscious level and are part of our automatic function like breathing. They get instilled early on and can stay with us a lifetime. Even being conscious of these emotions doesn't negate them. It is an ongoing process which requires discipline and focus.

Personally, I have been working on this for a while and am excited to be fortunate enough to get a seat in this six-week program and have a growth phase that begins after the six weeks. Nothing worthwhile is the easiest. Building new habits takes guts. I love this quote because at the end of the day we are the battery that drives us.

"The most important relationship you have in life is the one you have with yourself. Once you have that, any other relationship is a plus, not a must." —**Diane von Fürstenburg**

Our relationship, a relationship filled with love ♡🖤🤍, respect and trust, happens to be a must for me.

Good morning ☼! As I embark on my upcoming birthday, I decided to take stock of my life up until now and think about the decisions I have made or not made.

I happened to come across this quote from **James Clear**, which was very timely considering my current musings:

"One of the great mistakes in life is suffering for years because you didn't want to feel foolish for five minutes.

- *You don't want to apologize, so you let a relationship deteriorate.*

- *You're scared of the sting of rejection, so you don't ask for what you want.*

- *You fear people will say your idea is dumb, so you never start the business.*

Nobody likes feeling foolish, but the feeling fades quickly. The willingness to endure five minutes of discomfort turns out to be a meaningful dividing line in life."

Over life, we make millions of decisions big and small. I have made many great and worthwhile decisions in my life and taken on things that were out of my comfort zone and avoided decisions and committing to things that were out of my comfort zone or that became problematic.

This is human design. We do have self-preservation at our core. I also believe that we are limitless beings. Either way, don't let fear stop you from living your life, doing your ASK, stating your thoughts.

The best decision I ever made, which was definitely scary, was to be a parent and have you. I have never regretted it for one minute. ♡🖤🦓

Good morning ☀! Hope you slept well and deeply. I have been thinking a lot about the concept of taking back your power. It is crucial to seek to understand others, have compassion, and treat people fairly. It's also very important people treat you with respect, kindness, and with fairness too. At the end of the day, people will treat you the way you teach them to treat you. You have the power today to ensure people know how to respect you and know what your boundaries are. It is the energy you put out which is the type of people you will attract.

As a child, you were not in control of this because—grownups: parents, extended family, friends, teachers, and institutions—had control. And many times, words and actions are used that make kids feel less than and not worthy. I apologize profusely if I ever made you feel less than. I know this happened growing up in our home, and it came from insecurity and lack of awareness. It weighs on me. Today you are an adult, and you have complete control to choose what you want. So, take conscious action to make the most out of your life and be a leader for those around you. I love ♡🖤🦓 you very much and always want the best of everything in life for you.

Good morning ☀! A colder day in NYC, but we have been lucky this winter overall! I have been participating in a 4 Day Morning Challenge. Yes, I do have morning rituals, but I believe in improving and learning new ways to do things to find a more meaningful experience. The mind is the most open in the morning. So, the idea is to bring in positivity but also remove negativity. To find peace in the morning is important for the rest of the day. Regarding negative feelings and emotions, we tend to push them away, avoid them, or think that we need to "get over it." But often we just bury or ignore them so they linger and resurface in other places and situations. There is a method that is very helpful in dealing with negative emotions called the RAIN Method. Here is how it works. Take anger, for example. You can substitute any negative emotion such as fear, frustration, annoyance, unworthiness, etc.

R: Recognize what you are feeling. Name it: I feel Anger.
A: Accept it, acknowledge it, and allow the emotion to happen.
I: Investigate it with curiosity. Where did this anger start? Have I felt it before? Is there a pattern where I react in a particular way? What should I do? How often do I get angry?
N: Not Identify. This emotion is just a tiny aspect of me. It is not me; I will not label myself as an angry person or someone who gets angry fast.

When implementing RAIN, which you can do anytime you feel negativity, you take on an observer role to your emotions. You can acknowledge your feelings and see where it comes from, deal with it and then let it go. No more ignoring and stuffing it down until negativity becomes your default behavior.

As you recognize these feelings and emotions you can start to shift to the side of the brain that is transformative.

I love ♡🖤🫶 you and am always here for you.

Good morning ☼! Another Friday and a cold one, too!

I completed my 4 Day Morning Challenge today and it was definitely worth it. I realized that before I had a rote morning routine, based on what I thought I needed to do. This morning routine became a chore without any joy or embodiment. I have seven journals filled with affirmations and stuff.

Now I have a morning that works for me, that I can manage, and that brings me peace and vibrancy for the day. I am enjoying the morning and assigning true positive feelings to what I do at the start of the day versus what I thought I had to do. I want the same for you. To carve out time each morning to make it about you. To find a practice that works for you. A great thing to do is make an agreement with yourself in the morning, for example, an agreement that you won't check your phone or any electronic devices or make calls until a certain time in the morning. Try this for seven days and see how you feel and what you did during the time you would have been distracted by tech.

Bless yourself with the following thoughts:

May I be happy.

May I have strength in my body and mind.

May I live life with ease.

May I live life with kindness.

May I accept myself as I am.

May I be free.

I wish this for you every day. I love ♡🖤🩶 you with every fiber of my being.

Good morning ☼! Energy is one of my favorite things. We basically are energy beings, and this planet operates on energy frequencies, so I thought to share this list of habits that drain your energy so you can avoid and maximize!

Habits That Drain Your Energy:

1. Overthinking

2. Inconsistent sleeping patterns

3. Eating junk food

4. Living in the past

5. Negative people

This is probably the short list in life. I find your energy to be the best for me and I love ♡🖤🩶 it and you!

Good afternoon ☼! I hope you are having a wonderful day.

The things we say to ourselves, the self-talk, matters. It's not just thoughts that are a big part but the words that come out of our mouth.

I personally do not know if "I am . . . " statements make a difference. You can only change the program when you make the effort to rewrite it in the operating system. If the program stays the same, it will sabotage the best thoughts but at the end of the day, positive thoughts and words are way better than negative ones. I like pairing a slogan/command/direction that goes further than an "I am" statement and is in alignment with reprogramming the subconscious (operating system).

Here's one of mine: "I work smarter not harder, with less expectations and more grace towards myself and others."

I will come up with more.

Here is another one: "I love ♡🖤🤍 respect and adore my sons always and forever."

Good morning ☼! I hope you had a fun, restful, and restorative weekend!

Here we are heading to the Rosh Hashanah. A lot to think about as we embark on a new round spiritually and physically.

Wayne Dyer, a renowned motivational speaker, stated, **_"Don't believe every thought you have."_** So many times, we let a negative thought (thoughts become beliefs) run through our mind and they become our absolute truth. We actually seek out situations that sabotage us in order to reinforce these beliefs. They were formed in our early years and are part of our origin story.

So many times I yelled at you, said unkind and hurtful things. I hit also. My wrongs and mistakes caused feelings of lack, unworthiness, inadequacy, and conditional love. This is on me because it was my own frustration, inadequacy, and unworthiness that caused these reactions. It was not you.

I hope that at times I have come to you in the past and apologized for my actions. That I explained to you that my reaction was not due to you. If I did not, then I want you to know, right now, that I was not right in my head, and you are a treasure above all treasures. I want you to go into the New Year knowing how worthy, amazing, extraordinary and capable you are, and that you are loved ♡🖤🤍 unconditionally. These are the thoughts to believe going forward.

Good afternoon ☼! I just finished recording a podcast episode, and our guest said something very interesting that she called "Crushing the ANTS," which was developed by Dr. Daniel Amen. ANTS stands for Automatic Negative Thoughts. So how do you do this? You change the channel by:

1. Writing down the negative thought.

2. Ask yourself if it is true.

3. Ask yourself if it is 100% true.

4. Ask yourself how this thought makes you feel.

5. Ask yourself, "How would I be if I did not have this thought?"
    ♡🖤💚

Good afternoon ☼**!** I need to rethink how I spend my time or how productive I actually am if I am constantly on my laptop, phone, or desktop daily. Am I doing too many things? The answer is yes. Does all this work, effort, and business improve my quality of life? I honestly cannot answer that. Am I burying myself in busyness? Does it feed my need to achieve things even if it means just crossing things off an ever-growing to-do list? Truth is, I forgot a lot of what I take in because there are fewer brain cells to take in information. Plus, the mind naturally shifts through about 60,000 thoughts a day.

While I don't know if all this doing, nonstop, means anything, I know for sure is that I'll always have time for you. ♡🖤💚

Good morning ☼**!** I saw this quote on a friend's chat:

> **"Looking for consciousness in the brain is like looking
> inside a radio for the announcer." —Nassim Haramein**

Consciousness comes from G-d, a divine source. It's pure magic, limitless; so don't limit yourself to just the everyday thought. Pray, meditate, immerse in nature, ground in the earth. Open your mind to explore and connect with the grandeur of the force behind it all. There is an infinity of possibilities out there.

By the way, I love ♡🖤💚 you to infinity and beyond.

Good afternoon ☼**!** This week has been busy, and I decided to give myself a chiller day today. I'm working but at a slower pace and thinking about the Soul.

This Soul is G-d given and steers us correctly. People tend to avoid or disregard that voice in their head, but we are meant to embrace it. G-d does not waste anything in his creation of us.

Some people get confused between negative, sabotaging thoughts running through their head directing them. But this is not your intuition. Intuition is your internal knowing and the deepest wisdom we have access to.

As per Andrea Beaman, intuition is a natural ability that makes it possible to know something without any proof or evidence. You will know something without having to call to mind the reason you believe it. This is truth beyond any study you have read or the latest news story.

I hope you listen to your intuition and let it guide you. I know my intuition is very much connected to you. ♡🖤🤍

Good morning ☼! As we face challenges, remember it is not about what you did or they did, it's about how you deal with it and rebound. It is about what you learn and how much smarter you become because of it. It is where you see opportunity because you remain positive and optimistic even when you want to feel pessimistic or give up.

The brilliant **Rabbi Menachem Mendel Schneerson** on dealing with challenges:

> *"In every challenge or even tragedy, there is an opportunity. And if you train yourself to look for the opportunity, you will be able to take control of the situation and even turn it into a positive or if it can't be turned into something good, at least something good could come out of it."*

I will always be your backbone and I will always love ♡🖤🤍 you. I may not have the answers, but I believe in you and your will. G-d bless you.

Good afternoon ☼! I hope you had a marvelous weekend! I cannot believe it's already rolling into the second week of December—you can always tell when I'm not in the 5:00 am mode when I send my message after 12:00 noon.

Today, I am thinking about impatience and frustration. For sure, lack of patience leads to frustration, like when someone is walking slowly or taking their time. Being the New Yorkers that we are, this drives us mad. Or when we are explaining something, and the other person is not understanding or agreeing. Sometimes the other person is just asking questions for clarity. Triggers can cause negative reactions such as anger and impatience, and the best way to handle it is to breathe deeply and remember the action causing you to feel this way is irrelevant. It's what someone else is doing. How you respond to other people's actions, words, etc., is in your control. No one can cause or make you react. It's what you allow or don't allow. Your responses are within your power. To break these moments of frustration due to someone else, just pause, breathe, think of something funny, take a walk, or if it's someone you love, remember you love this person and will be patient. I know it's hard.

I'm a work in progress learning to be in the observer mode and react more with kindness than anger, patience than frustration.

> *"Someone being patient with you is one of the purest forms of love."* **—Unknown**

Sending you tons of love ♡♥🖤, patience, and kindness!!

Good morning ☼. I cannot wait to see you! This is my daily power message:

Here is my new mantra: Always go forward and not let excuses such as not having enough time, not enough connections, not enough knowledge, and not enough courage to hold me back.

I look back on my life and know that there was always a small step I could have taken—if I had the guts to take it.

> *"You can either be judged because you created something or ignored because you left your greatness inside of you. Your call."* **—James Clear**

I love ♡♥🖤 you and the greatness you clearly have inside of you.

Good morning ☼! I'm walking outside—had a few appointments and decided to walk. New York City is beautiful when the sun is out, and the air is warm. NYC is a walking city. I have been thinking a lot about life. I've been feeling anxious, troubled, and down lately. Having trouble with sleep, and the mornings are challenging again. I'm worried about reverting to my old mindset. But then I realize it's all a test, and the test is questioning myself and being vulnerable to self-sabotage in order to stop from moving forward. I am going forward.

I talk about the road to others, and it is time that I listen to it and share it with you.

> *"The road is long, and parts are messed up and full of potholes and parts are smoothly paved. Some roads are packed, and you can barely drive through, and some are wide and expansive; some have twists and crazy curves—that take you out of the way—and some roads are endlessly straight. Sometimes you come to a bridge, and the bridge is in disrepair, and sometimes it's brand new. The road, this journey, is our life. You have to be strong to stay on the road."*

I have to remember this. We are strong. I love ♡🖤🩶 you.

Good morning ☼! I love this quote. It is so simple yet so perfect:

> *"If you change the way you look at things, the things you look at change."* **—Dr. Wayne Dyer**

It always goes back to our thoughts and the emotions we tie to our thoughts. That's what shapes our perception of everything. It creates the energy level we vibrate at, and it's this energy we put out that tells people how to treat us.

So, if you change the way you think and look at things, things will change. Clearly, this is easier said than done.

I've been working on this for a while. G-d brings us mirrors all the time; a mirror is a person or situation that triggers a reaction.

But this person/situation is just on a mission to teach us. We need to acknowledge that whatever reaction we are having is exactly what we need to face and work on.

The goal is to eventually stop reacting altogether and take back our power. You're perfect in my eyes, but we all have to be self-aware and work on our reactions, thoughts, and emotions! I love ♡🖤🩶 you, and that's what is my thoughts always.

Good morning ☼! Guess what? I started working with a time management coach. I realized I have too many different things going on and am very distracted.

In addition, I am aging (but it's not a bad thing) and the cells in the brain holds less.

I decided to take the bull by the horns because I want to learn how to focus well on one thing at a time versus jumping from task to task which causes a loss of brain power and focus. I also want to be more intentional with how I structure my time and become more productive with less time invested.

The key is putting the phone away while I work on a specific thing and only looking at the inbox of that specific thing when working. When I remove my phone, my focus and efficiency go up dramatically. The phone is a mind killer (like fear) in a lot of ways.

I now have a schedule that helps build the habit of blocking time plus providing time for myself in between to eat mindfully and let my mind wander, which includes going outside.

You are at the right age to think about time management, organizational skills, executive functioning, and other skill sets that really help increase productivity and efficiency in a healthy way. You are probably already doing this to some degree.

But just like planning your financial future, your time is the biggest commodity after health so invest in managing it. Regardless of my time blocks, I will always take time to message you because you are always a major priority to me. My love ♡♥♥ for you has no bounds.

* * *

Reflection:
THE STRENGTH IN OWNING OUR STORIES

As I reflect on my journey of embracing accountability and mindfulness, I see it as one of my life's most challenging yet transformative chapters. Taking responsibility for my actions, owning my flaws, and acknowledging the ways I could do better wasn't easy, but it was necessary for me and for my sons.

In practicing accountability, I understood that leadership isn't about being perfect, especially as a parent. It's about being honest. It's about showing my sons that mistakes don't define us; what matters is how we respond, learn, and grow. I wanted them to see me not just as their mom but as a flawed and real human being committed to being better.

Practicing mindfulness taught me to pause, breathe, and respond thoughtfully instead of reacting impulsively. This transformed my relationship with my sons. They began to trust not just my love but also my sincerity, willingness to own up to my actions, and commitment to change.

My sons saw firsthand that accountability isn't about blame or shame; it's about empowerment. It's about realizing that we have the strength to take control of our choices, to be mindful of how we impact others, and to move forward with integrity.

To my sons, I hope you always carry this understanding with you. Life will challenge you, as it has challenged me, but remember, owning your story is the key to crafting a better one. Be accountable, not because others demand it, but because it's a gift you give yourself. Be mindful, not just for your peace, but because your actions will shape the world around you.

My wish is that these lessons inspire you to lead by example. Show your children and yourself that accountability isn't a burden but a strength. Mindfulness isn't just a practice but a way of living with purpose and presence.

CHAPTER 3

Dedication
Discipline

While I tried to teach dedication and discipline to my kids growing up, it was challenging because I would often walk away from a challenge or a goal, usually with negative self-talk. I definitely was not even consistent with consequences. However, reading books written by great thinkers made me realize that dedication and discipline are shared in every success story. No matter their background, they kept their goals and dreams and did not give up. I wanted to share with my kids that they can achieve anything. Over the past few years, my kids have seen me take on new projects and goals, including messaging them daily and authoring books. They celebrate my achievements just like I celebrate theirs.

* * *

Good morning ☼! I hope you're having a great one and that you had a great July 4th weekend! Your mornings are important because they set up the rest of the day. I heard this quote yesterday and really wanted to share it:

"There may be no heroic connotation to the word
PERSISTENCE, but the quality is to the character of a
person what carbon is to steel."

You are world-class; always remember this. Remember, too, how much I love ♡🖤🤍 you.

Good morning ☼! It's a beautiful day, and honestly, every day is a beautiful day when you wake up whole and healthy! How about just waking up?! Don't ever take that for granted. I was reading this quote from **James Clear** and thinking how often we just think of immediate rewards or the quick return and not about the longer wait, which can yield bigger rewards and may take more effort. I think today's technology and constant information flow on mobile devices and the pace of change over the pandemic have led to the idea of immediate returns on everything we do, or it becomes not worth doing. Maybe this type of entitlement or quick expectation is also a generational thing.

"We often make choices based on immediate outcomes.
What can I do to experience a little joy in the next
30 minutes? What can I accomplish in the next hour?
But if you always expect to get a little bit of reward for
a little bit of effort, then you often overlook actions that
lead to greater payoffs down the road. The relationship
between input and output is rarely linear. The course
of action that could provide greater happiness, meaning,
or satisfaction in the long run may not make you happy
in the next 30 minutes."

But this is okay because, at the end of the day, happiness is an inside job.

I send you everlasting love ♡🖤🤍 not just for the next 30 minutes or hour!

Good morning ☼! This week is flying with changes and new chapters for us all starting in August. We are fortunate, change moves us forward. We don't go backward; we move forward and learn along the way. And while we do not know the future, we do know how to live our best life in the moment.

I was reading about this young woman named **Forum Javeri** who lives in India. She attained the position of Director of the GIA Laboratory in Surat, India. She has hundreds of employees reporting to her. She worked hard with tremendous determination, thought leadership, and discipline to achieve this position in such a male-dominated culture. But when asked about her achievements, her answer is really noteworthy and a very good formula to follow for success:

> *"Don't work towards titles or positions; work for the love of what you are doing and learn along the way."*

The simplest advice is usually the most powerful. I love ♡♥🖤 you and bless you!

Good morning ☼! Installing great habits is the essence of living an abundant, legendary, soulful, and healthy life. As per **James Clear** in *Atomic Habits*:

> *"Breakthrough moments are often the result of many previous actions, which build up the potential required to unleash a major change."*

It takes work and commitment! Results have little to do with the goals you set but everything to do with the systems you follow ♡♥🖤.

Good morning ☼! You can do anything if you believe in yourself. Figure it out one step at a time, and every misstep is not a step backward but forwards because you learn from it. Watching you move forward gives me incredible joy, peace, and gratitude. It fills me up. Sending you love ♡♥🖤 and blessings and the power, strength, and burning desire to keep taking those steps and moving ahead.

Good morning ☼! Another Friday! Black Friday mania—we are barreling straight ahead to what will be a year for completion. This past year was a building year. I tend to send an even huger load of love on Fridays to cover the weekend. With all the bias and growing anti-Semitism that is at a peak in today's alarming cancel culture, I wanted to share this insightful and very on-point quote from **Cus D'Amato**, the legendary boxing trainer of Mike Tyson and other top fighters, on courage:

> *"I tell my kids, what is the difference between a hero and a coward? What is the difference between being yellow and being brave? No difference. Only what you do. They both feel the same. They both fear dying and getting hurt. The man who is yellow refuses to face up to what he's got to face. The hero is more disciplined, and he fights those feelings off and he does what he has to do. But they both feel the same, the hero and the coward. People who watch you judge you on what you do, not how you feel."*
> ♡🖤🤍

Good morning ☼**!** Another Friday! I wanted to share something I read today in Hero Manifesto by **Robin Sharma**:

> *"We've become a society of snowflakes, complainers, and hedonists who wish for only ease, pleasure, and luxury at every turn. Yet to do the towering work that stands the test of time and builds a life that you will ever be so proud of demands that you place yourself in harsh places. And force yourself to do difficult things so that the struggle introduces you to your hidden strength. And confidence. And brilliance."*

So powerful is this statement and so true. The greatest achievements tend to come from the struggle. And what's more amazing is the true masters don't stop once they produce that triumph—they don't rest on their laurels, fame, or wealth; they keep going because they want to bring more and learn more—they desire to go higher.

It's not about the money or fame; it's about being the best and continuing to bring it. FYI . . . Aristotle slept on a stone floor on purpose. I love ♡🖤🤍 you! You always make me proud!

Good morning ☼, and I was glad we were able to be together for dinner last night.

Never give up on your dreams. If something you believe in is not working, it usually just means revising or rethinking the plan. No person is ever whipped until he quits in his own mind. A quitter never wins, and a winner never quits. Always pick the best mastermind alliance you can find to surround yourself with and lead without needing a title or recognition. My heart is filled to the brim with love ♡🖤🤍 for you.

Good morning ☼, and guess what? As I embark on my health journey, I have committed to a 5-day water fast, which means only water! I am doing this. It is mind over matter. I have some hacks, which hopefully will help. I started last night, so this is Day 1. ♡🖤🤍

Good morning ☼! I am really blessed that we were able to be together for the Seders and to celebrate another Passover together. The idea of telling the story each year to the next generation loses its meaning when we are not together, so I'm grateful we were. It takes great discipline to stay committed to something.

Whether it is in maintaining traditions, following religion, doing your job, nurturing a relationship, or yourself. Inner character is where self-discipline lies.

> *"What lies behind us and what lies before us*
> *are tiny matters compared to what lies within us."*
> **—Henry David Thoreau**

This could not be truer because discipline, ethics, moral fiber, and character are the foundation from which everything else springs forth. Here is to always making sure we have it in us to be there for each other and stand up for what is right in an upside-down world. Be disciplined and committed to building a life filled with meaning, happiness, inspiration, and success. If this is the one thing I can pass on to you, then my life is a success.

I send you all my love ♡🖤🤍 and strength. May you have a swift Exodus from anything that holds you back.

Good morning ☼! I'm sending you an off-the-chart amount of love, peace, and positivity.

Remember, fear is just an emotion that informs you to gather more knowledge on a particular subject. Fear is a made-up story you get to recreate because it has not happened but is something projected into the future. Don't let this emotion paralyze you.

> *"Fear of failure is higher when you're not working on the problem. If you are acting, you are less worried about failure because you realize you can influence the outcome." —James Clear*

Don't let fear stop you, and know change gets messiest in the middle—so don't give up! ♡🖤🤍

Good morning ☼, my love! I hope you're having a beautiful start to the day. ♡🖤🤍 Whenever you are stuck searching for the optimal plan, remember that getting started changes everything.

> *"Motivation is what gets you started. Commitment is what keeps you going." —Jim Rohn*

And according to **Stephen Covey** of *7 Habits of Highly Effective People*:

> *"The main thing is to keep the main thing the main thing."*

Good afternoon ☼! I hope you are enjoying this glorious weather. I get that it's mid-June, but I'm always grateful for nice weather. So here is my message because I know you and everyone out there are all searching for something that you want:

- An apartment
- Job
- Lose weight
- Get into better shape
- Make money or make more money
- New or better relationships

- Better character traits

- Meaningful family connections

- Love

You name it; there is always something we humans want and are searching for. But we don't always get what we want or are searching for and then we get frustrated, upset, and give up. But I believe if you put the work in, you will get what is meant for you, what you need.

Just keep going because the day you stop searching for what you want is the day whatever you were searching for may finally be ready for you.

So, train your mind to see the good in everything you come across so you will not be frustrated and down when you don't immediately get what you want or are searching for. Be happy knowing it did not come your way for a good reason. Know that it will come to you when it is your time, and keep putting the effort in, keep going. One thing you will never have to search or wait for is my love ♡♥🖤!

Good morning ☼! I love ♡♥🖤 and adore you! I'm sending you positive energy, love, and serenity. EMPOWER yourself by saying the words "I CAN" in a place where you feel the belief. Say the words out loud as many times as you need to. Embrace your resistance and celebrate your victory.

DESIRE changes NOTHING . . .

DECISION changes SOMETHING . . .

But DETERMINATION changes EVERYTHING . . .

Have A DETERMINED DAY!

Good afternoon ☼! It's another wonderful Friday. A thought for the weekend:

> *"Life has no futile paths. Just shorter paths and longer*
> *paths. The longer paths lead to the highest places."*
> **—Chabad.org**

Those long-winding, uphill paths that make us want to stop and give up, those are the ones that will lead us to greatness. When we feel completely worn out, like we've been completely depleted, that's when we must get up, dust ourselves off, and show G-d, "We've got this." From there, he'll carry us through.

You also carry me through, and I hope you find I do the same for you. I love ♡💙🤍 you.

Good afternoon ☼! I hope this beautiful day is serving you! Because it's definitely uplifting! I hope you spend your time filling your mind with big visions and manifesting what you want, not squandering your mind with petty externally derived thoughts.

Once you return your mind to greatness and manifest your goals, dreams, and life vision, you will find you really don't have time for the pettiness, bullshit, gossip, and nonsense that seems to preoccupy most minds today. It's all over social media and comes through via people and media to distract you, to bring you down to the level of muck they live in. Misery loves company.

Don't go down that rabbit hole! Your dreams mean everything, and I support you every step of the way. Enjoy the weekend, and I'm sending you lifetimes full of love ♡💙🤍.

Good evening ☼! DAY 5. Just ended the fast, and I had to share this with you. This is so big for me, and the first person I want to share this accomplishment with is you. I can't believe it. Started Monday at 8:00 pm and ended Saturday at 8:00 pm. You know what?

I just broke the fast with soup but seriously was not even that hungry. MIND OVER MATTER. A big part of me wants you to be proud of me and to be a model of YES YOU CAN. I love ♡💙🤍 you and thank you for the support and encouragement over the past few days.

Good morning ☼! Another Friday, and just like that, the first week of the year is gone. "Hasta la vista, baby!" I think January is a "beginning" type of month. People are always setting resolutions, which usually don't stick. Changes do not happen without creating the supporting habits to make whatever goal you set attainable. This means taking on additional responsibility.

"Life rarely changes in a positive way without an increase in responsibility. That can mean taking ownership of your health or committing to a relationship or starting a business. Whatever it is, if you want the trajectory to change, the amount of responsibility usually has to change." —**James Clear**

What new goals and intentions do you have for the new year? What additional habits are you willing to establish to get there?

What additional responsibilities are you willing to embrace? All good food for thought, and if you need a sounding board, I am here! Sending you canyons of love ♡🖤🩶 and blessings always!

Good morning ☼! I hope your day is starting off beautifully! The sun is shining, so that is always a plus.

We started recording the Beyond the Table Podcast, where we discussed a topic with an expert. I have already recorded and edited 12 Spotlight Interviews. It's funny because not that long ago, the idea of a podcast would have been a "No!" I would have thought *I am not qualified, no skill set, nothing to talk about what*. The idea of it was intimidating and overwhelming. I felt clueless.

But I have learned that you cannot think like that because:

"Where you are at is determined by where you are headed, not by where you are coming from." —**Unknown**

I just practiced what I preached; take one step and then the next.

You are headed for greatness, and I am sure of this. Sending you love ♡🖤🩶, positivity, and blessings.

Good morning ☼! I hope your morning is starting off smoothly with gratitude and inspiration for the day! Since we are living in what one would deem as challenging times, I thought these words from *Atomic Habits* author **James Clear** would be helpful:

"You cannot remove struggle from life, but you can improve your ability to handle challenge."

"Two truths that can be at odds:

1. *There are no bonus points in life for doing it the hard way.*

2. *There is a lot to be gained in life by acting fast and giving your best effort.*

Don't let the excuse of searching for a better way prevent you from acting."

In other words, your ability to handle challenges, learn from them, and pivot while taking action and moving forward will give you leverage over your peers in seeing opportunities and capitalizing on them. I have no doubt in your abilities. I send you these messages to remind you of how smart, determined, and gifted you are. Always know this and be confident. I love ♡🖤🩶 you, and love is the engine always.

Good morning ☼! I hope you had a beautiful and restorative weekend. And just like that, we are in the second week of the year.

What's the plan for expansion? What do you have to do to get to the top? Well, you have to do what no one is doing! To quote **Robin Sharma's** brain tattoo:

"To have the results that only 5% of the population have, you must be willing to do what only 5% of the population are willing to do."

Here are some examples of what you must be willing to do:

- Work extremely hard: A solid work ethic beats natural talent.

- Sacrifice: If you love what you do, you do not feel like you are sacrificing.

- Install solid daily habits, which are core to good functioning.

- Deal with detractors: Do not let anyone bring you down!

- Look for solutions to challenges and learn from those challenges.

These are the "costs" to have what 5% of the population has. I love ♡🖤🩶 you, and "STAY THE COURSE."

Good morning ✡! I hope your weekend was restful and restorative and you took a break to give your mind a rest. I need to do this myself. I find it easier to give advice than take my own. I wanted to share this great quote about character:

> *"Life is raw material. We are artisans. We can sculpt*
> *our existence into something beautiful or debase it into*
> *ugliness. It's in our hands."* **—Cathy Better**

I find it takes more work and determination to stay the course and be a light, a leader, and a person of ethical standards than it takes to be what the majority of our peers/people are about these days. Always remember to go within and find that inner source, the divine spark, the strength to shine. Be the masterpiece and mastermind I know you are. Sending you currents of love ♡🖤🩶 every minute of every day.

Good afternoon ✡! Happy Purim and also Happy St. Paddy's Day! I was thinking a lot about Megillah Esther; it's the story of Esther. It's not called Megillah Esther and Mordechai for a reason. I think it's two-fold, which makes it a favorite story to not just me but everyone. You feel G-d's hand in this story because every twist feels divine. The fact that Esther saves the Jewish people with prayer, fasting, and real-time planning, comes together in triumph.

The story also shows us women are strong and can do whatever it takes. G-d definitely wanted this message out because he knew that for generations into the future, the world would remain upside down in that women have been defined by men.

My favorite line is when Esther is hesitant about going to the King, even with knowing the annihilation of her people was in the works. Mordechai asks her, *"Why do you think you are here? You were made queen for just this moment."*

Those words make her act, and she does so decisively. This is what we must remember. We are here for a reason, don't let fear stop you from your purpose. **George R.R. Martin** said:

"Fear cuts deeper than swords."

Don't let fear cut you down. You are a big reason why I'm here. I love ♡🖤🤍 you and wish you a joyous day!

Good morning ☼! Let's examine what I call the 3 Ds, which are central to who we are. The 3 Ds are foundational—either you have them, or you don't, or you have some combo in your makeup.

The 3Ds are Determination, Discipline, and Doing.

By doing, I don't mean tasks and being busy for the sake of being busy, but doing that leads to achieving plans and goals you set monthly, quarterly, and yearly.

My constant goals are:

1. to always be there for you;

2. to be present in your lives;

3. to not be a burden;

4. to live my life's vision.

I rely on the 3 Ds to make my goals a reality.

D #4 is love. Love is not duty. I choose to love ♡🖤🤍 you from the bottom of my heart and soul.

Good afternoon ☼! Where is the day going? I was thinking about this because I find myself losing time during the day and I realize it has a lot to do with distractions and being able to focus. If there's a single key to success or an impediment to success if you don't have it, it's the ability to focus like a laser on whatever it is you're doing. It's definitely a human condition that we are challenged at establishing and focusing on our priority.

We are addicted to distractions from our phones and tech plus the constant adding of tasks to our to-do lists. It is more efficient to visualize the three things that you want to accomplish in a day and focus on it and say no to anything else.

Pick three things that will move you forward and make you stronger personally and professionally. Do the hardest thing first in the morning when you are fresh. Say no to things that are not in your wheelhouse.

It is not selfish; it is actually selfless to say no. I have a hard time saying no to you. And I also know that I should have on many occasions. It is one of the hardest parts of being a parent and loving ♡🖤🩶 too much.

Good morning ☼! I was so happy to have the chance to stop by this morning after my podiatrist appointment. I'm always so impressed by you and your brother. How you made this beautiful apartment even more beautiful and turned a place into your home. You acted and you always continue to do so, and it really delivers.

While I was thinking about this, I came across a quote that I wanted to share with you as we enter Q2. Author and screenwriter **Ray Bradbury** on the power of cumulative action:

> *"Action is hope. At the end of each day, when you've done your work, you lie there and think, well, I'll be damned, I did this today. It doesn't matter how good it is, or how bad—you did it. At the end of the week, you'll have a certain amount of accumulation. At the end of a year, you look back and say, I'll be damned, it's been a good year."*

I am proud of your bravery and the action you take. I love ♡🖤🩶 and admire you.

Good morning ☼! Can you believe this is the week leading up to Memorial Day weekend and an unofficial start to the summer? I can't. It's like time is on super-fast forward. So, I am going to think about what I want to do this week and get it done.

What about you? Do you have anything you say you want to do?

Carl Jung put it very succinctly:

> *"You are what you do. NOT what you say you are going to do."*

But there are those who believe that if you think, believe, and say it enough, you will manifest it. So, I guess you have to do all of the above to make it happen.

I hope your day and week is as beautiful as you are! I love ♡🖤🩶 you!

Good morning ☼! It's known that champions have a different attitude and mindset than others.

They don't give up; they have a dream and always move forward. They have discipline, they train, they practice, they learn, they do not put off what they have to do. They do not procrastinate; they do not talk themselves out of their vision. They not only physically practice but mentally rehearse their moves. Those at the very top of the field map every move in their head and practice it over and over which wires neural pathways to create the reality they want. They are not afraid to fail; they learn and keep going. It is an inner drive.

This quote sums up what it takes to be a champion. It's all about the recovery.

> *"I really think a champion is defined not by their wins but by how they can recover when they fall."*
> **—Serena Williams**

You are a champion. I know it and love ♡🖤🤍 this about you. Remember who you are.

Good morning ☼! Here we are—Friday. Passover is around the corner.

I have been thinking a lot of the significance of Passover and all of the extreme challenges and shifts that have been coming for a few years but are culminating since 10/7. It is insane that we are still asking to let our people go. I am firm believer that G-d gives us all tests that we can pass. Tests are NOT easy. Typically, it is often opposite to our personality, mindset, experience and skill sets, and this is why it is hard. It is hard because we feel fear.

Every single one of us will go through tough, incredibly hard things. This is life. **Earl Nightingale** said, *"No obstacle can take you out."*

We all have the capacity to overcome and come out stronger, maybe even set ourselves free. We always have each other. This is love ♡🖤🤍.

Reflection: THE POWER OF SHOWING UP

Reflecting on the journey of dedication and discipline, I realize how much these values have shaped the legacy I leave for my sons. What once felt like insurmountable challenges became growth opportunities when I committed to showing up for myself and my family.

Dedication taught me that dreams don't need to stay dreams. They become reality through consistent action, even when the road is difficult. Discipline taught me that success isn't about perfection; it's about persistence and moving forward even when doubts creep in or obstacles appear.

In living these lessons, I've grown not only as a person but also as a parent. My sons have watched me take on challenges I once avoided and turn them into victories both big and small. They've seen me finish projects, achieve goals, and celebrate progress. Most importantly, they've seen me live out the message I've always tried to teach them: *You can achieve anything you set your mind to.*

The beauty of dedication and discipline isn't just in our achievements, it's in the habits we form, the character we build, and the inspiration we provide to others. My sons' joy and pride in my successes remind me that our journeys are never ours alone. When we commit to growth, we uplift those around us.

To my sons, I hope you always carry this truth with you: the path to your dreams may not be easy, but it will always be worth it. Dedication will guide you when motivation fades, and discipline will steady you when challenges arise. Celebrate every step forward and never underestimate the power of simply showing up.

I hope this chapter inspires you to embrace your journey with renewed purpose. Show your children the strength of commitment, the resilience of discipline, and the joy of celebrating progress.

CHAPTER 4

Mindset Wisdom

Mindset has become a huge buzzword. As you can see in this book, I quote thought leaders, visionaries, leaders, and geniuses because their words helped me rethink my function. I realized that everything in our mind from the time we are born shapes our perception of reality. Visionary Wayne Dyer said, *"Change the way you look at things and the things you look at change."* When our intentions become positive and we search for good, we can transform our life into something powerful and unique. I learned this at age 59, so I decided to share it with my kids immediately and keep reinforcing it. I started messaging daily in the first place simply to share the wisdom I was learning by reading and doing many programs. I found it all fascinating and vital. I realized that schools do not teach mindset, positivity, or true wisdom in many ways. They do not always empower kids to feel truly worthy. I understood that if I accomplished one thing, it would be to let my kids know how worthy they are and how much I love them. I believe parents can influence their children's mindset and teach them to have a growth-oriented perspective. When developing wisdom over time, it is valuable to encourage kids to think before they act, consider others' feelings, and make thoughtful decisions. Ironically, this wisdom is not taught or considered part of being wise.

* * *

Good morning ☼! What is the difference between mindfulness and mindset? These words are buzzwords that are commonly used.

Mindfulness is a passive practice that allows us to pause and observe (our habitual thoughts) with curiosity. Mindset is the active practice of identifying depleting thought patterns and replacing them with positive thoughts that are more supportive and compassionate of ourselves. So, the passive practice leads to the active practice.

Breakthrough moments are the result of many previous practices and actions which build up the potential required to unleash a major change. When we really feel and believe we are successful, we align with being successful. I send you immense love ♡♥🖤, positivity, energy, healing, and gratitude for you being in the world.

Good morning ☼! Remember, there is always a fresh start. Each day you wake up is a fresh start. Today is another Women Beyond the Table call. Every month the group meets is truly a milestone. Who would have thought? This is the beauty of life; there are unknowns, so all we can really do is take a step. And then, before you know it, the steps have become a block, and the blocks have become a mile, and so on. It's movement, not stagnation, which brings you forward. Thinking of you brings me warmth and joy. Sending you my deepest love ♡♥🖤, adoration, and respect. Sending you multiple rounds of blessings.

Good morning ☼! Another weekend is here! Back in the day, fear was so real. An animal could attack you. Being away from your tribe meant zero protection; the elements and starvation were very real things. Today, feeling fear is still important to keep you from doing something dangerous or life-threatening or to get you away from harm really quickly. However, today, people are staying in a constant adrenaline-infused stress state which the body reacts to with the same fear reactors. Fear holds us back. So, it's important to not let your fears control you but to have the right internal dialogue where you are in charge. To be the sovereign who commands the subconscious so you will reach your goals and potential.

> *"Courage is not the absence of fear or despair, but the strength to conquer them."* —Danielle Steel

My love ♡🖤🤍 for you is a fearless thing.

Good morning ☼, Starshine. "The Earth says 'Hello.'" That was a song from the 70's—I'm sure you can tell.

I don't even remember if those are the right words. But it feels right for the earth to say good morning along with me. Remember, the countdown to a new year begins. Don't let anybody waste your time. Be intentional about your time and who you spend it with. Get aligned with your goals and be brave enough to make new choices.

You are my sun, stars, and moon, and I love ♡🖤🤍 you.

Good morning ☼! It's another Friday! Crazy how fast the week goes. When a ship is on the sea, the sea does not overrun the ship. It sails. The only time the water takes over the ship or sinks it is when it gets inside the ship. This is how negativity works. It gets inside you from the outside and takes you down. Don't let anybody or anything in that will take you down inside. Positivity is the way. Surround yourself with positive thinkers.

Sending you yachts, ships, and tankers full of love ♡🖤🤍.

Good afternoon ☼! I hope this beautiful day is serving you! Because it's definitely uplifting, and it's Friday—a 2 for 1 joy bringer! I saw a great line from **Robin Sharma** in *Hero Manifesto*:

> *"Fill your brain with giant dreams so it has no space for petty pursuits."*

Once you return your mind to greatness and manifest your goals, dreams, and life vision, you will find you really don't have time for the pettiness, bullshit, gossip, and nonsense that seems to preoccupy most minds today.

It's all over social media and comes through via people and media to distract you, to bring you down to the level of muck they live in. Misery loves company.

Your dreams mean everything, and I support you every step of the way. Enjoy the weekend, and I'm sending you lifetimes full of love ♡🖤🩶 and blessings!

Good morning ☼! I was determined to get back on track and send this message early so you could feel my love and positive energy all day long. What I wanted to share was something really next-level I heard from the workshop. In the workshop, the leader discussed an interview that he did with guest **Peter Crone** who is a mindset coach to top athletes, CEOs, etc. The question to Peter was, "What is your advice on getting to the next level?"

Crone answered, "Everyone's goals are too small. It's not just creating a vision but expanding on it. You have so much more in you than you think. People tend to expand linearly. They apply logic to progression. They go from point A to point B; instead of going linear, go VERTICAL. Expand your vision up. Think exponentially and expand in every dimension. Think very big, and when you do, your mind will tell you what it takes or what you need to do to make big happen.

When you think small, just to the next linear point, your mind only seizes on this next point and does not show you how or what you need to think or do to get way bigger. Become what you want to be NOW."

I have no doubt you are wired to think exponentially. I love ♡🖤🩶 you and love that about you.

Good morning ☼!

> *"Life is a journey that can be magical or mundane.*
> *We are the ones to choose."* —Alena Chapman

Such a simple statement but very powerful. When we are children, we feel the magic, the essence around us.

We imagine and see things and live in a multi-dimensional world. However, we lose that ability as our families and society shape us with rules, dos and don'ts.

What really happens is we lose the magic. The magic is in being open to your soul and hearing it. It is being open to the wonders of life and the universe and living it.

So, I say choose the magical journey and rejoice. I love ♡🖤🩶 you through every soul journey I have ever been on.

Good morning ☼! Ahhh, the last day of November. I want to share a story of resilience and not giving up. ♡🖤🩶

The inspiration is **J.K. Rowling,** the first novelist to become a billion-aire. Her vision for Harry Potter came to her while she sat on a delayed train to Kings Cross station in London. The idea for all 7 books and the central theme for Book 1 came to her on the train. It was a blazing, intuitive message—the boy who doesn't know he's a wizard goes to wizarding school. She wrote the book on scraps of paper. Book 1 was written at a cafe while she was a single mom on welfare. Her mother passed away while she was writing, which caused J.K. to go into a depression.

However, she did not stop writing and used her emotional darkness to build her characters. On completing *The Philosopher's Stone*, she sent 3 chapters to prominent literary agents, and only one replied. She received many rejections from publishers who said the book would not be commercially successful or interesting to young audiences. Bloomsbury finally agreed to publish *Harry Potter and the Philosopher's Stone* but asked Joan Rowling to add a K after her first initial (Kathleen is her middle name) because they felt a feminine name would turn off the target audience of young boys. That's how she became J.K. Rowling.

Even after she became the bestselling author of all time, she didn't walk around thinking she was all that. Her goal remained to "write better than yesterday."

As a matter of fact, she published a crime book series under the name **Robert Galbraith**. Without revealing her true name, she sent the book to publishers for consideration and received many rejections, plus the suggestion that "a writers' group or courses may help."

The moral of the story is:

- Put the work in, and do not give up.
- Don't make excuses to abandon your work or goals because it's tough, challenging, or because of external/environmental events.

- Stay humble.

- Always strive to improve.

- Someone's opinion is just someone's opinion. Do not believe it if it doesn't serve your ascent.

"Fall down seven times. Rise up eight." —Japanese Proverb

Good morning ☼! Beautiful day and slightly warmer—I'll take it! Well, I am excited because tomorrow is Thanksgiving, and I get to spend the day with you and our family. I was reading some posts yesterday, and one really grabbed my attention:

> *"We don't see things as they are, we see them as we are."*
> *—Anais Nïn*

This simple statement has stayed in my mind. We look at everything through our own prism. Everything we see is based on where we in at a particular moment in time, and much of this is based on the past: our childhood, past lives, beliefs, culture, family story, peers, society, and things we pick up along the way to the present.

So, it makes me wonder if we ever actually see reality or just what we want to see. One truth I know is that you are the best thing that ever happened to me, and I love ♡♥🖤 you for real!

Good morning ☼ to the best! I was going back through some quotes and readings that impacted me, I don't think I shared this before, but it's just so touching and true:

> *"Sometimes you have to remind yourself you*
> *are something special; you cannot be replaced.*
> *Your heart, your conversation, your care,*
> *it cannot be replaced by anyone."* —Unknown

You are extraordinary, one of a kind, and never replaceable.

I love ♡♥🖤 you to the moon and back, to the sun and back, and across the galaxies.

Good morning ☀! Sorry for the delay today! Had more time to charge the love batteries! I'm the luckiest mom to always have you to love, adore, and cherish. As you embark on today's mission, know that:

> *"We cannot predict the value our work will provide to the world."* —**James Clear**

That's fine. It is not our job to judge our own work.

It is our job to create it, to pour ourselves into it, and to master our craft as best we can. Here is another thought for the day from **James Clear**:

> *"The way someone else perceives what you do is a result of their own experiences (which you can't control), their own preferences (which you can't predict), and their own expectations (which you don't set). If your choices don't match their expectations that is their concern, not yours."*

My concern is for you and your happiness. I love ♡🖤🤍 you so much.

Good morning ☀! So today is day 4 of my group water fast, and I hear it gets better at night. I definitely slept better, but not feeling great this morning! This, too, shall pass. I heard a great tip on one of my calls yesterday. Put the state of being you want to be in NOW. State your intentions in the present. When you think about your future, think of the person you have become, the achievement, the accomplishments of future you, and FEEL the emotion of future you NOW.

I send you love ♡🖤🤍, peace, and blessings. You mean the world to me now and always.

Good morning ☀! Finally, the sun is back in West Palm Beach. Yesterday it was rainy and 60 degrees! NYC was 44 and sunny. But I was still grateful and happy to be here! Then I realized everything in life really depends on how you look at it.

You are where you are for a reason, and that is to look around and see the possibilities and the beauty and create memories and new pathways in the mind.

There are no coincidences. Nothing is a problem, only if you see it and believe it to be.

"Use your eyes to see the possibilities, not the problems."
—Unknown

I love ♡🖤🩶 you and see your limitless potential and possibilities.

Good morning ☼! I cannot believe it's another Friday! It's Monday, and then it's Friday. I love this quote from **James Clear**:

> *"Being pleasant and having a good attitude is a simple*
> *way to become luckier. Opportunities come through*
> *people, and people are more likely to bring opportunities*
> *to people they like. It's hard to win if your attitude adds*
> *friction to every interpersonal experience."*

It's simple, nice, good people don't always finish last. Where did the "nice guys finish last" statement even come from? Money is wonderful, but it's the byproduct of the value you bring to people and nothing more.

So, think of what you can do to make someone's life better or easier, and do it with a smile and open heart because it will come back to you many times over!

BTW. . . a wealthy person is not the person with the most money or possessions; it's the person who is loved, confident, and has good health, happiness, and positivity. It is the person who is accountable, the observer in control of their emotions.

I love ♡🖤🩶 you *"to infinity and beyond."* There I go again, quoting from the great philosopher, **Buzz Lightyear**.

Good afternoon ☼! I was on Zoom from 7 am–12 noon! But now I'm walking outside, breathing, and each hour that goes by that I don't send my morning message weighs on me! You know I am a big fan of instilling good and positive habits. The smallest improvement you decide to implement can produce massive changes. I try to always add that 1 small positive improvement and repeat it daily to produce a change. The funny thing is that this concept—philosophy—has ancient roots. But then again, it is the tried-and-true stuff that works.

Our ancestors and the ancients were very smart people!

The ancient Greek poet **Hesiod** on small improvements:

*"If you add only a little to a little and do this often, soon
that little will become great."*

I love ♡🖤🩶 you, and may you go from strength to strength!

Good morning ☼! I really love the concept of the "start." Each morning
is a fresh start. It's such an amazing concept we take for granted. To think
you get a new start every day and a new start every Monday, a new start
every 1st of the month, a new start each year.

There is always an opportunity to start something, do something differently, or learn something new. Always have gratitude for this and appreciate this incredible chance G-d brings to you continually. And each
time you take advantage of this tremendous fresh start opportunity; you
will see promise everywhere. This is where the true change happens.

"Change is the end result of all true learning."
—**Leo Buscaglia**

Sending you love ♡🖤🩶 and blessings every morning, every day,
week, month, and year!

Good morning ☼, and I hope your day is starting off great! I'm reading
Think and Grow Rich by **Napoleon Hill**. It's amazing and as relevant today
as when he originally wrote it in the 1930s. I am going to combine a few
quotes in this message because they are powerful and connected.

*"Fear is a habit, so is self-pity, defeat, anxiety, despair,
hopelessness and resignation. You can eliminate all these
negative habits with two simple resolves: I can, and I
will. When you close the door of your mind to negative
thoughts, the door of opportunity opens to you. There are
no limitations to the mind except those we acknowledge.
Both poverty and riches are the offspring of thought."*

Negative thinking, habits, and emotions were a thing back then just
like they are today. You must be willing to go beyond and rewire your
brain as soon as negative thoughts and emotions come in. I can promise
you that when I am thinking of something not positive for me, I change my

thoughts by thinking of you. The feeling of love ♡♥🧡 that comes over me washes out any low feelings and bad thoughts.

Good morning ☼, and remember, everything is all in the way you look at it: Point of View!

> *"Different meanings can be assigned to the same events. Look for evidence of how the world is encouraging you, and you will find it. Look for evidence of how the world is burdening you, and you will find it. Choose an explanation that empowers you."* —**James Clear**

I am going to put this into practice. The evidence states that I love ♡♥🧡 you completely, and that is a fact that encourages me greatly.

Good morning ☼! Another summer day is upon us! I was reading the final pages of *Think and Grow Rich*. It is definitely a book that transcends time. **Napoleon Hill** states:

> *"If you fail to control your own mind, you may be sure that you will control nothing else. Your mind is your spiritual estate; protect and use it with care to which Divine Royalty is entitled. You were given willpower for this purpose. Without a doubt, the most common weakness of all human beings is the habit of leaving their mind open to the negative influences of other people."*

This is why I tell you that you are remarkable, extraordinary, worthy, capable, and disciplined—a masterpiece. You are divine, and these are the thoughts you must have and hold in your mind. So, either you control your mind, or it controls you. A practical method for controlling the mind is the habit of keeping it busy with a definite purpose backed by a definite plan and not open to or dependent on the influences or judgments of others. I love ♡♥🧡 you and your vision.

Good morning ☼! Here are a couple of thoughts to start your day:

> *"When you control your thoughts, you control your mind.*
> *And when you control your mind, you control your life."*
> —**Robin Sharma**

> *"Man can only receive what he sees himself receiving."*
> —**Florence Scovel Shinn**

Remember the power of your thoughts; you can control your thoughts. I love ♡ 🖤 🤍 you from the bottom of my heart, and I see you receiving it all!

Good morning ☼! Sending you a tanker full of love. During my morning meditation, I heard a very interesting way of looking at things by Synctuition. It involves changing your perspective. Ask these questions:

"Are you a positive or negative type of person? Do you see the glass as half empty or half full?"

The way you see things is the perspective or angle you are looking from. If you always look from the top down, the glass will always look full. Take the high view and always look at things from the highest angle!

> *"We are what we repeatedly do. Excellence then is not an act but a habit."* —**Unknown**

Remember always, every minute of the day, you are world-class, you are a legend, and I love ♡ 🖤 🤍 and believe in you.

Good morning ☼, and I hope your day is starting off smoothly. As I think about the state of the country and beyond, I find myself thinking about my circle of concern. According to the legendary **Stephen Covey**, author of the *7 Habits of Highly Effective People*, we have a circle of influence and a circle of concern.

The circle of influence is what you can influence, while the circle of concern would be out of your control, i.e., politics, world events, big tech, all media (news, print, online, social, even what is streaming nonstop), movies, etc. You get the idea. Everything wants to send you messages or tell you what to think. It is full-speed and aggressive. But you have a superpower, and it is called your mind. You have power over your thoughts, and thoughts affect us both physically and spiritually.

I know you are a fan of **Marcus Aurelius**, so I found this quote from him, which I think speaks to the heart of this:

> *"You have power over your mind—not outside events.*
> *Realize this, and you will find strength."*

My love ♡🖤🩶 for you is a powerful and strong thing.

Good morning ☼! As I think about the weekend, I realize it's kind of trivial with a war going on in Europe—the madness of it all, along with the talk of bringing in nuclear capability.

It seems like the Europe of your grandfather, a Holocaust survivor, and your great-grandfather, a Sergeant in the US Army fighting in World War 2, is far away. 80 years ago, but it's here again. I pray for the innocents in Ukraine and Russia who are caught in this tragic situation. I worry about this useless US government and the fact that this war could have been avoided. How stupid. Sending you all my love ♡🖤🩶, and I'm filled with gratitude that you are safe.

Good morning ☼! Spring is here, and a thought came into my head about something that is rather full circle for me. I recently saw the remake of the movie *Dune*. Back in HS, I read *Dune* by **Frank Herbert**. It is a masterpiece, and I did not grasp the deep meaning in the book back then until the new remake of the movie *Dune*.

The new version was really well done as opposed to the version done in the 1980s, which was somewhat of a joke. The book has many elements that are completely relatable today. I was reading today, and out of nowhere was this passage from *Dune*. I felt like it was a message to me as I had been thinking about the remake I saw.

> *"I must not fear. Fear is the mind-killer. Fear is the little*
> *death that brings total obliteration. I will face my fear.*
> *I will permit it to pass over me and through me. And*
> *when it has gone past, I will turn my inner eye to see its*
> *path. Where the fear has gone there will be nothing.*
> *Only I will remain."*

This applies to our lives daily. We face the fear of trying, fear of failing, fear of succeeding, fear of not being enough, imposter syndrome fear, fear of loss—you name it. But know this; it has no power, only the power you give it. And remember; never fear that you are not loved ♡🖤🤍, admired, or adored. You have everything and more; G-d is with you. Know this; believe it, and you will SOAR.

Good morning ☼! Countdown to our family vacation, and I cannot wait. With the times being what they are: uncertainty, big challenges, and huge changes in every area of life, it may feel cliché, but there is always a way to rise above. Yes, you must think out of the box. But there are always solutions and opportunities. You have to be open. You have to open your mind vertically and exponentially, bypass linear, and see possibilities.

> *"Believe it can be done. When you believe something*
> *can be done, really believe, your mind will find the ways*
> *to do it. Believing a solution paves the way to solution."*
> **—David J. Schwartz**

My solution is resilience, faith, and love. My love ♡🖤🤍 for you is a constant that moves me forward.

Good morning ☼! I am on my way to Long Island for a hike, lunch, and then back to the city. I'll do some work on the train back and forth. My daily gift to you is inspiration and sharing things I learned or read. Here is the mantra of the day:

> *"You can have anything you want if you are willing to give*
> *up the belief that you can't have it."* **—Dr. Robert Anthony**

I want you to be happy first and to believe you can have anything you want and be whoever you want. We are the only thing that holds ourselves back by making excuses for why we cannot have or be. Remember this.

You're the best "have" in my life. Having you as my son is everything! I love ♡🖤🤍 you.

Good morning ☼! You know what is liberating? The realization that:

> *"We are only one decision away from changing our minds."*
> **—Teresa Vozza**

I was sitting virtually at a round table on Monday, talking about recession-proofing. Big topic today! Basically, the statement means we are not trapped. We should not feel trapped that we cannot make a decision to change a path. Our decisions can change everything. Bulletproof your mindset, and don't lose sight of your goals or ability to shift and keep going forward. Short-term focused people lose sight of the bigger picture.

You are my big picture. I love ♡🖤🩶 you, and I think love is a primary key to bulletproofing our lives!

Good morning ☼! As we usher out the year let's have a plan and philosophy for the new year: Don't look around, look within!

> *"When you need to learn quickly, learn from others.*
> *When you need to learn deeply, learn from experience."*
> **—James Clear**

When dealing with stress, remember that most of your stress comes from the way you respond, not the way life is. Try to adjust your attitude and try to change how you see things. Try to look for the good in all situations. Take the lessons learned and find new opportunities.

For me, if you can manage stress, live the plan above and incorporate a new philosophy, I will be the happiest mom alive! I love ♡🖤🩶 you and wish you a great year.

Good morning ☼! I hope you are having a great week so far.

I have been thinking about emotions. My emotional state fluctuates, and I notice it is a common thing. Emotions can affect how you see everything and how you feel minute to minute. It's quite amazing how emotions can be triggered and rule us even. Most of the time we start feeling a certain way by someone or something that is nothing to do with us but triggers an emotion that is tied to some past event. Or we bring up a past memory that triggers an emotion.

It's not easy to hold back, literally stop, identify what you are feeling, make the emotion, understand and observe it, and then diffuse it and see the scene for what it is.

I want to share a quote of his that kind of incorporates my above thoughts:

> *"A memory without the emotional charge is called wisdom."* **—Dr. Joe Dispenza**

I wish for you the ability to not let emotions impact and make choices for you, but I do hope you feel love and gratitude always. I love ♡🖤🤍 you deeply.

Good afternoon ☼! Every day is a new day to rewire your mind and create new neural pathways and disconnect hardwired pathways by stopping a negative thought from the past. Mentally rehearse whatever you want for yourself, then associate a feeling with this vision of gratitude and joy and you will be far ahead of the curve. Champion athletes mentally rehearse every play in their heads over and over and feel the energy of the play being a success.

Know that you are loved ♡🖤🤍 immensely, and I have gratitude and joy for you being in the world every second and minute of the day.

Good afternoon ☼! Today is hump day, and I hope your week is going great!

We are all focused to a degree in getting what we want. Some of us know that if you just measure what you want based on subjective or external KPIs, you may always feel a lack.

According to **Dr. Joe Dispenza**, you need to *"Break the habit of being yourself."*

Instead of stating things like, "I can't believe it," and "Why does this always happen to me?" You can be asking yourself, "How can I think, feel, and behave differently to produce the effect/result that I want?" Reframing your thoughts will move you to a state of consciousness that allows you to connect to a universal intelligence, make direct contact with a field of possibilities, and send a clear signal that you expect to change and see the results produced in your life. My wish for you, at your age, is to be able to mentally rehearse and visualize your future self today. Connect within to make it a reality. You are the key and have everything you need.

You are always part of my consciousness and the thought of you brings me the strongest and deepest feelings of love ♡🖤💚, joy, and gratitude.

Good morning ☼! I have been working to stop any thoughts or reactive feelings that I realize are part of a subconscious program running decades. Do thoughts produce feelings or do feelings produce thoughts?

Truth is, over time it becomes a loop where one triggers the other and vice versa. This is the mind (thoughts) body (feelings) connection. It runs deep. You have to change both, go in deep and reprogram your operating system (not for the faint of heart). The program dates back years, so since I had a hand in putting it there, I feel these messages are my way to bring you insights now so that you can create your reality to be whatever you want it to be, because you are limitless. You have to believe it. I love ♡🖤💚 being able to see you thrive.

Good morning ☼! As we go into the Jewish New Year and ask to be written and inscribed in the Book of Life, keep this in your mind: How healthy you are is up to you.

So yes, it's about great food choices. Sugar is evil. The flour today is completely modified. Use spices and herbs and infuse more plant-based alternatives into your daily living.

Exercise but not anaerobic exercise which the brain does not like and neither do your joints.

Stop or cut down drastically on wine, liquor, smoking, vaping, cigarettes, pot, drugs.

But the secret sauce to rewiring neural pathways and increase regulation of healthy genes is through our thoughts, our mind.

Change the negative thoughts. Shut them down, because they do shut your brain down. Over 90 percent of health is well within our control. G-d designed us with everything we need to not only self-heal but live a long life.

Sending you tons of love ♡🖤💚 and blessings for great health, happiness and abundance!

Good morning ☼! I am looking forward to getting away this weekend. Taking a break from the city and changing locations seems very good for my head.

As I was thinking about this, I also realized that there are ways to feel like I am someplace else right around me. There are things that I can do and explore without the expenses of a flight and hotel.

It's all how you look at it. It's called being resourceful.

"Now is no time to think of what you do not have. Think of what you can do with what there is." —**Ernest Hemingway**

You are what I do have, and that is everything. I love ♡🖤🤍 you. Have a blessed day!

Good morning ☼! I hope your day started off smoothly and is full of promise.

Sometimes we don't feel like there is much promise or progress or light at the end of the tunnel.

It's easy to say, "Think differently," or, "Change your mindset." But in reality, it's not always possible or easy when we are in the midst of dealing with something that is trying.

There is an old **Japanese proverb** that says:

"If you feel like you are losing everything, remember trees lose their leaves every year, yet they still stand tall and proud and wait for better days to come."

May your tree always stand tall with deep roots. May your leaves and fruits be abundant. You are the best and I love ♡🖤🤍 you more deeply than the deepest root!

Good morning ☼! A friend sent me the book *The Four Agreements*, by Don Miguel Ruiz, with which I was not familiar. It seems like good and very basic advice. Sometimes it's the basic, obvious advice that is hardest to accept.

1. Be impeccable with your word.

2. Don't take anything personally.

3. Don't make assumptions.

4. Always do your best.

Four rather obvious and simple statements! Then why are these things so challenging for most of the people in this world?

My main agreement is to always love ♡🖤🩶 and adore you.

Good morning ☼! Wednesday is hump day and a great marker of time. It's the middle and once you're over the hump, it's Hello Weekend!

Question: Do you think Nike got its ingenious tag line "Just Do It" from this quote?

Journalist and author **Flora Rheta Schreiber** on starting before you feel ready:

> *"You're never ready for what you have to do. You just do it. That makes you ready."*

Nike coined "Just Do It" in 1988. Rheta's work came out in the 70s, but it's possible this quote was said later on in response to her bestselling work.

Regardless of who came up with it, don't wait. Just take the first step and that will get you to the next step and provide the motivation for each step that follows. We are never 100 percent or even 50 percent ready, are we? Doing is a mindset, so just do it! Follow the path and don't be afraid to take a step. I believe in you and have great faith in your brilliance. Sending mountains of love ♡🖤🩶 your way every day.

Good morning ☼! I am feeling good, being honest and real with myself. No delusions.

Maybe it comes from not creating this little box of thoughts in my head that things need to be this way, or done only that way, or that I am not doing enough. Perhaps the concept of "standing in truth" just comes from being fluid and not rigid in thoughts, expectations, and whatever everyone else thinks and says is the "right way."

I'm a big fan of former **President John Kennedy**, and when I saw this quote, I knew I wanted to send it to you.

> *"What does truth require? It requires us to face the facts as they are, not to involve ourselves in self-deception; to refuse to think merely in slogans."*

You are my truth. You are everything real and good, the best there is. ♡🖤🤍

Good morning ! According to Neural Linguistic Programming, 95 percent of what we do is subconsciously driven. The five percent consciously driven part of the brain can make "I Am" statements all day and promise to make changes but if the subconscious is not on board, then there will be no change, and self-sabotaging behavior will continue. No matter what you promise yourself.

To change, we have to reframe the way we view and perceive things because the subconscious is driving how we interpret what we see. It's the story we tell ourselves and the context we put things in. The goal is to integrate the conscious and unconscious and align them so that you can see things differently or without the preprogramming.

> *"When you change the way you look at things the things you look at change."* **—Wayne Dyer**

It sounds so simple, doesn't it? But it is not simple because our programming has been running for years. This is why I try to be accountable and work hard on my reactions and perceptions. It's constant work, and I have up and downs. But know that it is my love ♡🖤🤍 for you that pushes me to keep trying.

Good afternoon ☼. This morning, I was posting about Holocaust Day and remembering my father, your grandpa, who went through hell on earth and torture not that long ago. I don't honestly know how it made it, survived, functioned, and built a life, even while experiencing additional immense challenges such as death of a son (my brother) and divorce. But he moved on and always found happiness and peace. He had that type of mindset, to always keep going and find the good. I can tell you that grandpa would be devastated to see what the world has become and what is happening in this country today. That the world has not learned. You are part of a strong, vibrant, brilliant legacy. You are everything and more. You will lead. ♡🖤🤍

Reflection: A LEGACY OF WISDOM

Reflecting on the journey of wisdom and mindset, I see it as one of the most profound gifts we can pass on to the next generation. Wisdom is not something we are born with; it is cultivated through experience, reflection, and the willingness to learn and grow. Mindset is not fixed; it is a daily choice, a lens through which we view the world and ourselves.

The shift began when I realized how much power lies in our thoughts and beliefs. The words of the many visionaries whose books I started reading lit a spark within me, showing me that when we change how we think, we change how we live. This realization came late in my life, but it arrived at just the right time to share it with my sons.

Daily messaging became my way of weaving these lessons into my sons' lives, not as lectures but as small, steady reminders of their worth, potential, and the importance of having a growth mindset. My hope has always been to instill in them a deep sense of worthiness and self-belief, to remind them that they are not defined by mistakes or limitations but by their ability to grow, learn, and create.

Wisdom is not about knowing everything; it's about being thoughtful, considerate, and open to seeing the world through new perspectives. I wanted my sons to understand that being wise means thinking before acting, considering the impact of their choices, and navigating life with compassion and integrity.

To my sons, I hope you carry these lessons with you always. Remember, the world will reflect what you believe about yourself, so choose to see yourself as worthy, capable, and powerful. Let your mindset guide you through challenges and shape a life that is uniquely your own.

My wish is that you feel inspired to cultivate wisdom and a positive mindset in your and your children's lives. Teach them that they are enough, just as they are. Share the knowledge and insights that have shaped your journey; those lessons are treasures they will carry long after you're gone.

CHAPTER 5

Fulfillment Purpose

I was listening to a TED Talk by the brilliant Johann Hari, author of *Stolen Focus*. He spoke about depression and said that depressed people feel disconnected and as if they are lacking purpose. This made so much sense to me. When people think their lives have meaning, they are less stressed, cope better, and seem happier. Purpose drives people to wake up enthusiastically and know their efforts contribute to something bigger. Fulfillment is the reward for staying on your path and persevering. I saw my dad go to work six, sometimes seven days a week. He worked extremely hard, but he never expressed a love for what he did; it was his work. He owned a business and was a great businessperson, but I cannot remember him saying this was his passion; it was more like what he did every day.

After my parents divorced, my mother worked many jobs to earn a living. Earning money was the focus, and it was not easy; however, she reached a level of purpose and fulfillment when she decided to get her BA at age 54, which had a tremendous effect on her. I went to college and took a job because that was what was expected, to make money and become independent. My parents were not going to pay for my apartment and support me. I got my MBA not because I was passionate about business but because I thought it was a good move. However, it was not until I started messaging my kids that I began to feel a sense of fulfillment and purpose. Messaging was not one-and-done; it was a habit I built, and every message gave me an incredible feeling. I also became very aware of the growing concern that many young adults feel less fulfilled and lack a clear sense of purpose. So, I wanted my sons to know that it is more important that they are happy and love what they do, get out of bed with a sense of purpose, and are passionate about their work and well-being.

*   *   *

Good morning ☼! We all have an exit date, and if all the people who passed were in a room with us, do you know what they would say? "What are you waiting for?" Live in the moment and make every day a 10! Don't wait to start something. My questions to you are, "What can you do to make your day a 10, and how can I make your day a 10?" I love ♡♥♥ you and am sending a blessings list longer than I can type!

Good morning ☼! Another Monday, the first Monday of February. I am fortunate to have taken this vacation, as it is truly glorious to wake up with the sun shining, a view of the water, and palm trees outside. It brings a lightness of spirit and a good vibe. It is a great way to start the day! I would be remiss, though, to say I don't also appreciate crisp, cool air where you need a sweater and coat but feel alive. Crackling with energy! So, clearly, I like the balance. That's my life vision, to have the ability to have the best of both worlds. Warm balmy weather most of the year and the ability to break it up with other seasons and weather. Another thing to balance is our physical, emotional, spiritual, and intellectual lives. You must take care of your mind, body, and soul daily to have balance to have a fulfilled, healthy, and happy life. We all know this intrinsically, but most people don't keep on top of all these important areas. Why not? I would say it's because it requires effort, commitment, and consistency.

But in truth, it starts from the thoughts we have, which can either motivate us to do or procrastinate indefinitely. It really comes down to our thoughts and beliefs. So, step 1 is to look inward at your beliefs and thoughts and recognize what you need to work on and change. One thought, one element, one new habit creation, to create a small win and go from there. Everything we see is brought to life by a process of thinking. And thinking is a choice.

> *"All that we are is the result of what we have thought. The mind is everything. What we think we become."* —**Buddha**

To my Buddha! I send you the power of the sun, the warmth of my love ♡🖤🩶, and the blessings of the creator of it all!

Good morning ☼! It is always astounding how fast time is moving, at least to me it is. I am old enough to remember when Zoom was used to describe movement. Zoom is such a common word in today's virtual world that it seems old-fashioned to use it in its dictionary meaning: flying by, moving, or traveling quickly.

What I am saying is that time is zooming by, and so is life. Do we have time to fulfill our destiny, our dreams, create, and build? How about embracing our life vision? Remember, there are bumps, rubs, issues, and challenges that come up quickly and often in our zooming lives. But no matter what the time frame on Earth, know this:

> *"The difficult is what takes time. The impossible is what takes a little longer."* —**Fridtjof Nansen**

I love ♡🖤🩶 you regardless of time, space, zoom, or lifetimes.

Good morning ☼! I hope you had a good weekend. I am participating in Lifebook, which is an amazing personal growth course, and I heard this last night while doing the course. I wanted to share it with you because it is very impactful. **Jon Butcher** shared this in his recording. Some say that John Lennon said this quote (which has been disputed), but there really is no definitive answer as to who came up with this gem, only that it remains unsourced. People have used parts of this quote as something they claim to have said while growing up:

> *"When I was little, my mother told me the most important thing in life is to be happy. When I got older and was in*

school, the teacher asked us what we wanted to be when we grew up. I answered 'happy.' The teacher said that I did not understand the assignment, and I said, 'You do not understand life."

This really is the most important thing, and it's what I want for you. To be happy. Happy with yourself, happy in what you do, and happy in who you are. You make me happy always, and I love ♡🖤🩶 and adore you.

Good morning ☼! I wanted to share this quote, something to keep in mind, to stay centered and be you because you are awesome:

> *"Being yourself is a continuous effort. There is always another expectation placed upon you, another person pulling you toward their preferences, another nudge from society to act a certain way. It's a daily battle to be yourself, not merely what the world wants you to be."*
> **—James Clear**

I love ♡🖤🩶 you, and I hope you love yourself too.

Good morning ☼! The earth says, "Hello!" I was thinking that BC (Before COVID)—and during the beginning of COVID—I got up later in the morning and started working around 11:00 AM, did my thing, and was pretty much done by 7:00 PM unless I was traveling. I watched TV and binged series. Now I get up earlier, do not watch any TV, and I have to force myself to stop working or doing some tasks by 8:00 PM. I have lists and feel very busy all day, but the question is, "Busy doing what?" Am I busy with things that further my goals and move me closer to what I want, or just being busy? Am I progressing with quantifiable outcomes or just completing tasks? I guess this is the question for the ages!

Jim Rohn states it perfectly and is truly something to be aware of in our "busy" lives:

> *"Don't mistake movement for achievement.*
> *It's easy to get faked out by being busy.*
> *The question is: Busy doing what?"*

I have to think about performance measures!

Raising you kept me very busy, but guess what? I loved ♡🖤🩶 every minute of it, and you are extraordinary!

Good morning ☼! It's Friday! How was your week? Did you enjoy it? Was it productive? Did any moments stand out? Did you take the time to smell the proverbial coffee? Did you feel full and happy?

It seems that we go through time but don't really appreciate it or see the miracle of just being able to experience each day; to be honest, it can change in a blink. We take for granted getting up, working, doing what we do in peace, and having resources and convenience available to us regularly.

The thing is, as humans, not only do we pass through time—it flies past us—but we often repeat the same cycles of behavior repeatedly. Imagine if everyone woke up each day and said, *"Today I'm going to be a better person; today I'm going to do the right thing; today I'm going to have gratitude, appreciate, and celebrate being on Earth; today I'm going to cherish myself, my family, my neighbors."* How would we change time, and how would we change history? Would it rewrite itself? What would our future look like?

Deep Thoughts by **Jack Handey**—that's me, your mother, LOL.

One thing I very consciously committed to each, and every day is appreciation and gratitude to G-d for my life. For being born in a country where I have been able to live freely and have opportunities to grow and prosper. To have the most wonderful kids any mother can ever hope for and to know what love ♡🖤🩶 is because of the love I have for you.

Good morning ☼! I am enjoying a later day in bed, which is always nice and welcome. I have not been to a comedy show in years, but I am so glad we got together, bought tickets, and went for it. The show did not disappoint, and laughing and hearing your laughter was the best. Laughter is a huge gift and apparently has all these physical and psychological benefits. Living life, doing what makes you happy, smiling and laughing, and feeling joy are musts.

I think laughter on a regular basis is as important as air, water, sleep, and food. So, work hard but laugh as often as possible, too!

I love ♡🖤🩶 you a lot. You are my joy bringer!

Good morning ☼! I want to say how wonderful you are. It warms my heart that you honor your grandparents and remember them, that you engage in learning and prayer in their name. There is no higher elevation for their soul and yours when you do this.

It is such an achievement to be remembered and honored after one passes away. KUDOS for doing this for your loved ones!

> *"Trust yourself. Create the kind of self you will be happy to live with all your life. Make the most of yourself by fanning the tiny inner sparks of possibility into flames of achievement."* —Golda Meir

Never sacrifice 3 things: your family, your heart, or your dignity. You are creating the kind of life you will be happy to live with all your life. I am so proud of you and love ♡♥▨ you for being who you are.

Good morning ☼! Yesterday flew by, and I did not send a message! Oy! Women Beyond the Table had its official 1-year, 6-month call. Yes, as a young network, we celebrate half-birthdays! But as I was leading the call, I realized that no matter how much time, energy, and effort I put into this group, I get way more back. That's the secret sauce. Whatever you decide to do, wherever you work, whatever project or new road you take, make sure you are willing to serve, but doubly make sure you get way more back. It's not just about money; it's about loving what you do and the joy of doing it. It's about relationships and connections. The money comes when your head is in a good place. I send you lots of love ♡♥▨, positive energy, and blessings always.

Good morning ☼, my brilliant son! I love you! Here's a great insight from **Paul Graham**:

> *"The more you let a single belief define you, the less capable you are of adapting when life challenges you."*

And another from **Deepak Chopra**:

> *"Place your intentions in the vast ocean of all possibilities and allow the universe to work through you."*

My love ♡♥▨ for you is as vast as the ocean.

Good morning ☼. So many people are looking to find themselves. They don't know who they are or what they want. They don't know their strengths/weaknesses, nor how to capitalize on or minimize them. They don't know who to surround themselves with. I guess that is why **Aristotle** said:

> *"Knowing yourself is the beginning of all wisdom."*

As we prepare to enter a new year, take the time to really know yourself and be willing to fail and learn. Figure out what's working and what's not. What habits are giving you gains, and what habits are detracting from making gains? Try putting the year's positives and negatives on paper. It's not a matter of right and wrong, patting yourself on the back, or berating yourself. It's just an observation/analysis of the year, what you learned, what you did, and what you need to elevate and work on, and then get to it.

I love ♡🖤🤍 you regardless of what's on the positive and negative list. I'm your biggest cheerleader. You are limitless. Believe it and go for it. Kick fear in the ass.

Good afternoon ☼ from OK City! I am at a conference. I gave my speaker presentation and had the opportunity to attend very educational sessions. One that stood out was the Keynote given by **Marcus Lemonis**. He said something I wanted to share because it really resonated with me, and I believe is the purpose of being in business:

> *"I got into business because I had something to prove;*
> *I stayed in business because I had something to give."*

I will add that:

> *"Money is the byproduct of the value you bring."*
> **—Unknown**

Embrace these words, and you will always be a success. Work hard, give, provide value, and bring the love of G-d into all you do too. I love ♡🖤🤍 watching you succeed.

Good morning ☼, to my sunshine. Sending you blessings and much love ♡🖤🤍 as always.

As we go through the High Holiday New Year Cycle, we think about what we want in the New Year. This quote struck me when thinking about new habits to install and goals for each quarter:

> *"Life is easier when you know what you want—but most people don't take the time to figure out what they want. It's not that we are completely lost, but our efforts are often slightly misdirected. People will work for years and ultimately achieve a lifestyle that isn't quite what they were hoping for—often, simply because they never clearly defined what they wanted. An hour of thinking can save you a decade of work."* —James Clear

But then I thought about what **George Bernard Shaw** said in response to the mindset that many in the population believe *"money is the root of all evil."* Shaw said, "Lack of money is the root of all evil." I agree with that; it is the lack. People operate from a lack mentality, a scarcity mentality. When you operate this way, you set your future in writing. So, let's be affirmative and be in an abundant mindset. There is no lack ♡🖤🤍. Or, as **Neo** of the *The Matrix* said:

> *"There is no spoon."*

Good morning ☼! Today, I started reading *The Path of Me*, written by Wendy Hutchinson. She opens the book's introduction with the following quote:

> *"Somewhere buried deep within each of us is a call to purpose. It's not always rational, not always clearly delineated, and sometimes even seemingly absurd, but the knowing is there. There's a silent something within that intends you to express yourself. That something is your soul telling you to listen and connect through love, kindness, and receptivity."* —Dr. Wayne Dyer

So don't mask your emotions and think you have to wear armor and project an "image." Let who you are shine and be your authentic self. You can be sensitive to boundaries and empowered with compassion.

Always listen to your inner voice but do the continual work of personal and spiritual growth to make sure your inner voice is not stuck in the dogma of your earliest years when limiting beliefs are made.

I love ♡🖤🩶 you. Please forgive me if I contributed to the dogma limiting beliefs.

Good afternoon ☼! I'm energized and pumped up. I'm sending this energy to you to pump up your day:

> *"What are the two most important days in your life?*
> *The day you are born and the day you figure out why."*
> **—Mark Twain**

Short but very impactful quote. Most people do not know their "why" and live an entire life not knowing. It took me a while to figure out my "why" and I can tell you that you and your brothers are a big part of it. I love ♡🖤🩶 you and the WHY ladder!!!

Good morning ☼! I hope you had a wonderful and restorative weekend. I was thinking a lot about accomplishing and achieving; expectations placed on us by family and society. But I realize it's really an inside job. It's much harder to achieve when the expectation is demanded externally. It's internal. To truly achieve, you must be free; you have to know what you want. Then you take control of yourself and let G-d show you the way.

> *"No man is free who is not master of himself."* **—Epictetus**

I love ♡🖤🩶 you and bless you with every breath.

Good morning ☼! Another Monday, the last one of January, and just like that, we are moving into another month in a new solar year!

I was thinking about happiness. What is happiness? Is it a state of mind? What triggers it? Is it something that requires an external happening or thing to occur? Is it generated inside? Is it just the release of dopamine—what makes dopamine happen? Is it thoughts or a certain mindset? Is it a particular connection? I honestly don't have an answer because it's probably all intertwined and a case-by-case thing. I know for me, thinking of you, knowing you are happy and safe, brings me happiness. Love brings me happiness. Security and accomplishment bring me happiness. Doing, traveling, and learning brings me happiness. Self-respect and success bring me happiness. And abundance brings me happiness. Here is a quote from **Mahatma Gandhi** that resonates with the concept of happiness:

> *"Happiness is when what you think, what you say, and what you do are in harmony."*

At the end of the day, some people spend their lives pursuing happiness while others create it. A study of people who lived past 100 yrs. revealed one thing they all had in common. They had great senses of humor and laughed a lot. They saw and created joy daily. It was not their diet or whether they exercised but how they looked at life. They chose to laugh and be happy. Choosing happiness is way better than choosing stress. Trust me on this!

I wish you a lifetime of laughter, happiness, and love ♡♥❤.

Good morning ☼! It's officially another new month! Before you know it, we will be heading into a new season. I am so glad you are in your new apartment and enjoying the excitement of it.

I feel like this is a time of change for all of us. I feel I did something right that two of my sons want to live together! A time of true promise and growth. So, I just wanted to say hello to new chapters and, live smart, true, and remember to smell the roses. I love ♡♥❤ you and will always be here for you.

Good morning ☼. Speaking of certainty, of having a feeling and knowing that you are on the right path, you have to keep going, flowing, and moving. You must go there. No doubt, no hesitation.

I love this quote by journalist **Hal Boyle** on certainty:

> *"What makes a river so restful to people is that it doesn't have any doubt—it is sure to get where it is going, and it doesn't want to go anywhere else."*

I have no doubt about you. It is a certainty that moves me along.

Good morning ☼! For a parent the most important and constant thing you want for your child is that they are:

Healthy

Safe

Happy

Did you notice that safety comes before happiness?
As you grow, the list grows in that you want your kid to:

Be a good person.

Have values and ethics.

Being a leader.

Find their path.

Complete education and initiatives.

Make their way successful both professionally and personally.

Live well.

Be independent.

Then the list grows again:

Find a wonderful spouse.

Have amazing and healthy kids.

Live a long life facing tests and challenges with ease along the way.

You have already achieved the majority of these things, and this is why I feel so blessed and fortunate. I stand in awe of each of your accomplishments and achievements, and in the kind of man you are. Thank you for being an amazing and incredible son and human being. My love ♡🖤🩶 for you knows no bounds.

Good morning ☼! A college student once asked the **Lubavitcher Rebbe Schneerson** what is his job. The Rebbe gestured to the ceiling of his room and replied:

"Do you see that light bulb? It is connected by wires to an electrical generating station that powers the whole of Brooklyn. And that plant is connected to turbogenerators at Niagara Falls that power the whole of New York State and more. Every one of us is a light bulb wired in to an infinitely powerful generator. But the room may still be dark, because the connection has yet to be made. The job of a Rebbe is to take your hand in the dark room and help it find the switch."

It is all of our jobs. You are my switch and light. Love you ♡🖤🤍.

* * *

Reflection: LIVING A LIFE THAT MATTERS

As I close this chapter on fulfillment and purpose, I am grateful for the clarity this journey has brought me. Purpose isn't about grand gestures or monumental achievements; it's about finding meaning in the ordinary and every day. It's about infusing passion into daily life. It's about waking up with a sense of direction, knowing that what you do matters, no matter how small it may seem.

For much of my life, I misunderstood this. Like many, I believed that fulfillment was tied to external success, titles, or financial stability. But as I reflect on my parents' lives and my own, I realize that true fulfillment lies not in what we do but in *why* we do it. It comes from aligning our actions with our values and letting our passions guide us.

Messaging my sons became my *why*. What began as a small act of connection grew into a source of profound joy and purpose. Each message reminded me that I was contributing to something bigger: my sons' understanding of themselves, their worth, and their ability to live meaningful lives.

To my sons, I hope you carry this lesson with you: Fulfillment is not a destination; it's a journey of living authentically and intentionally. Whatever path you choose, let it light you up, making you excited to face each day and leaving you with the deep satisfaction of knowing you've made a difference.

My wish is that you find and nurture your sense of purpose. Purpose doesn't have to be loud or flashy; it can be found in the quiet moments, the simple connections, and the impact you have on those around you. Fulfillment is the reward for living a life aligned with your heart.

When we live with purpose, we enrich our own lives and inspire others to do the same. Know that what you do matters and that the world is better.

CHAPTER 6

Growth
Personal
Development

My quest for growth and personal development jumpstarted my desire to communicate more with my kids. While the pandemic was challenging and scary, it forced us to stop. Everything was shut down, and it was a time for many of us to reflect and look inside. I had been working hard and traveling nonstop from 2014 to March 2020. Work was the only place where I felt a sense of worth; traveling was an escape, and I also enjoyed seeing new things and feeling free. Because of my mindset then, I was also judgmental, defensive, frustrated, and competitive. I had a great fear of losing my work because I needed the income to support my sons, and fear is genuinely the "mind killer." Immediately at the start of the pandemic, everything changed, and although I wanted to panic, for some reason, I thought G-d wanted me to take a good look at the fact that I was not okay or happy. I thought, "What can I do?" What I did was immerse myself in personal development. I hired a life coach and business coach, and I read and committed to programs and coursework. This kept me busy and gave me a sense of purpose and fulfillment because I took care of myself. My self-worth increased because I was learning and growing instead of being a victim. I was gaining a better understanding of myself. Expanding my knowledge, skills, and perspectives resulted in more confidence. I understood I could adapt, overcome obstacles, look back on challenges, and see them as gifts.

It was so liberating that I decided to share the importance of personal development and learning and growing with my kids. I wanted them to understand that the minute they think they know everything, it is the end. We are here to learn and grow. As my kids saw me change and navigate challenges and life more effectively, they saw the truth in my messages and the ability to attain lifelong success. I genuinely believe that parents play a pivotal role in fostering growth and personal development in their children.

✧ ✦

Good morning ☼! Hope you enjoyed the weekend. A fresh new week is upon us, and a new month! Your strongest muscle is your mind. Nourish it very well with the healthiest foods that are high in nutritional value, take in plenty of air, breathe deeply, and drink 8–12 glasses of water daily. Remove social media, news, booze, smoke, drugs, and indoctrinating media, and replace them with books, learning, and decoding of negative beliefs.

Open your inner eye, use your instinct, and listen to your intuition. When you do these things, the subconscious, which controls trillions of cells, will become your servant instead of you serving it. Your conscious mind will be the true king and become open to the universe. You will be in a better state of flow.

> *"Your strongest muscle and your worst enemy is your mind. Train it well."* —Lise Gottlieb

Sending you a ton of love ♡🖤🤍 and flow!

Good morning ☼! I thought to share with you a great message I saw downtown on the street. Funny how these messages keep popping up—I know it's G-d giving us reminders. I'm sharing it with you to give you a big dose of positivity all day. "Learn to love who you are becoming."

I love ♡🖤🩶 who you are endlessly!

Good afternoon ☼! You know what weighed on me? That I did not get my morning message to you!

You are most important, and that means getting my message of love, inspiration, and knowledge to you. Here's some knowledge and inspiration: your thoughts matter, so pick ones that will up-level you and bring good energy. Writer and suffragist **Lucy Mallory** on the power of thoughts:

> *"Every thought a person dwells upon, whether he expresses it or not, either damages or improves his life."*

Know that even on the days I may miss sending a message, I'm proud of you and will always be proud of you. I love ♡🖤🩶 you with all I am.

Good morning ☼! Ah, it's Dec 1. Last month of the year. Can you believe it? Since COVID entered our world, its life in a different world. The jury is out if the world is getting better or worse. I am not a judge. The question remains the same: Are we learning? Each lifetime you live, you are supposed to learn to fulfill a soul contract. Learn to shed vices and embrace love, charity, faith, and compassion. This is how your soul moves forward. That's the everlasting part; this is what makes us immortal. Our soul continues. But remember when you live life, that:

> *"It is not about waiting for the storm to pass.*
> *It's about learning to dance in the rain."* —**Vivian Greene**

I have loved ♡🖤🩶 you in every lifetime we have shared and those to come.

Good morning ☼! I hope your day is starting off smoothly; no bumps or early-day challenges to navigate. What I like to do is not look at my phone at all for the first hour or so upon rising. I don't read messages or emails; I just do what feels right. By not looking at the phone, I don't get distracted by messages, emails, social media, news, etc. These distractions and indoctrination, in many ways, are designed to take away your cognitive ability, set you up for some type of mood, raise your cortisol, create anxiety, or even bring rage.

It is possible the message is humorous or good news, but at best, it's a distraction from doing the positive habits that set you up for a positive day. The phone has a way of derailing the focus needed to take steps closer to your goals. I love ♡💙🩶 you to the moon and back—actually across the galaxies and back.

Good morning ☼! I'm sending you lots of positive vibes mixed in with lots of love. I am reading *Conversations with G-d* by **Neale Donald Walsch**, and this quote jumped out at me:

> *"Life begins at the end of your comfort zone."*

Refusing to change and grow is the most unsafe place to be. Be patient with the process of change because it is disruptive to break down old foundations and build new ones. Change = DIScomfort. But remember, something new and beautiful comes out of it.

Master your mind = master your life.

> *"When you control your thoughts, you control your mind,*
> *and when you control your mind, you control your life."*

I have sent this quote from **Robin Sharma** previously because it is spot on. I love ♡💙🩶 you and know that your mind is amazing.

Good morning ☼! I really loved ♡💙🩶 seeing you yesterday! You make me so proud. I cannot tell you enough how much I love, admire, and respect you. You blew me away with your charitable giving. We will have the best year, a year of ascension.

I am going to work hard to understand my emotions and enter the observer state and continue to grow and network. You are my North Star, and we go onward and upward always.

Good morning ☼! I hope your day is starting off smoothly, even if it's not, even if there are challenges or setbacks. Let's face it: Challenges are part of life. Going forward means being open to going back a few steps, too. Why? Because there are learning curves everywhere, and we need to experience it all to become better thinkers and strategists. You did this on a regular basis when you were a baby, toddler, child. You learned and grew. It's no different now. Don't think the tasks are more difficult now because you're older. You faced the toughest tasks when you were little (standing and walking is TOUGH). That's the beauty of being human. We get challenged, we experience, we learn, we get smarter. We get fresh starts to do it all again, and we keep going until we succeed.

I watched you fall down many times, and each time you got up with that determined look on your face, I worried (I'm a mom and hated watching you fall), but I celebrated you getting up. I love ♡♥🖤 you!

BTW . . .

> *"When a child is learning to walk and falls 50 times,*
> *they never think to themselves, 'Maybe this isn't for me.'"*
> **—Mindset Made Better**

Good morning ☼. I hope you had a restful and restorative weekend! I have been reading the *Tao Te Ching*, which is a series of meditations on the mysterious nature of the Tao—the way, the light—the source of all existence. It was compiled in China 2500 years ago. Accordingly, the Tao is found where we least expect it:

> *"Not in the strong but in the weak,*
> *not in speech but in silence,*
> *not in doing but in not doing."*

Pretty interesting! Being a doer myself, it sounds intriguing. There is a different topic heading on each page and the Taos view/take on that topic. I'll share some over the week. I love ♡♥🖤 you every WAY!

Good morning ☼ **to you!** Remember, you are strong, you are worthy, you are capable, you are a money magnet, you are the absolute best, and you are always evolving. The greatest measure of intelligence is how intelligently you live your life. It's not a score; it is not how smart you are. It is how smart you live and think. I love ♡♥🖤 you to the moon and back.

Good evening ☼! Never thought I would let the day go by and send my message so late! It was a good day because I finally took time for myself. My friend came into the city, and we had a great lunch and walked around. Lately, I seem to spend most of my day between my desktop, laptop, tablet, and phone. Even your father is like, "You're still in front of a computer?"

I find I start early, and between my business, our restaurant, and Women Beyond the Table, I'm working all the time and not taking any quality time—just the morning hours.

I realized I'm messaging you about distractions and taking the time, you need to breathe and give your brain a break, and I am not doing it myself. I also experienced a deep sense of gratitude for the simple act of getting outside and walking, breathing, and enjoying a nice lunch with my friend. Today people in other cities and countries don't even have that. They can't walk around and meet friends and enjoy themselves because of war and danger. Another thing I thought about was how grateful I am that we all are so blessed. But most of all, I feel so blessed you are okay and living your life and that you are happy and well. I also really appreciate the beautiful things you do.

I love ♡🖤🤍 you and will get back on earlier messaging tomorrow!

Good morning ☼! I was on the road at 5:45 AM, and now we are less than an hour away from Newport, RI. It's important to take a day to do something nice and out of the box. It does not have to be a big-ticket thing, just something as simple as being in nature and being with someone you enjoy, or being by yourself and daydreaming, or trying something new.

The point is to honor and value yourself. Make the space and time to nurture and care for yourself. Your body and mind will be better for it and thank you by performing at a higher level.

I'm finding this mindset of valuing myself has carried over into other areas of my life, both on the professional and personal side. I love ♡🖤🤍 and value you!

Good evening ☼! This is a late one. It's so strange with this 5-day water fast. I was up at 4:00 AM with some great ideas flowing. Then I fell asleep at 6:00 AM. Your father woke me at 8:00 AM—he wanted to make sure I was okay. He checked on me and called a few times today and yesterday to make sure I was okay. I started this fasting journey on Monday at 8:00 PM, so finishing day 2 soon and going into day 3. I'm keeping positive that I can do this. It's my equivalent of running a marathon. But marathons screw your joints up, and 5-day fasts once a year lower your risk of cancer by 90%, and your body literally gets rid of the toxic cells and forces you to produce new cells.

During these fasts, your energy goes to repairing your body.

I love you! Even fasting, my love ♡🖤🖤 for you, is a very clear thing in my mind!

Good morning ☼**!** Another Friday, and it feels like it was just Friday! I messaged previously about setting boundaries and when you should be saying NO. Funny how synchronicities work because I was listening to someone on a podcast yesterday, and they said, "You become what you say YES to."

Fascinating! We do have to say yes in certain circumstances. For example, when learning a new skill set and starting in a new role. Remember to be cognizant as you level up to what truly serves you and is in alignment with your growth.

This is up to you. There are boundaries you set for your professional life and your personal life.

Hard work does often include saying yes when you are on your career journey, so use good judgment always.

No boundaries when it comes to LOVE. I love ♡🖤🖤 you!

Good morning ☼**!** This morning I was thinking that my mood may be a cause and effect of the holidays, seasonal transitions, or the full moon and portal we just passed through, but here is my thought: Sometimes, after being in certain environments or around groups of people, or just one person in particular, I feel an energy drain, and I don't know if it's me or just the people/person around me—but do you ever feel this? That you outgrow your surroundings and or the pettiness and judgmental nature of people. I saw this quote I thought was interesting. It's a good approach to life and people in general. A sort of vaccine or inoculation against the assholes out there!

"When they judge you, yawn.
When they misunderstand you, smile.
When they underestimate you, laugh.
When they condemn you, ignore.
When they envy you, rejoice.
When they oppose you, prevail."
—**Matshona Dhliwayo**

Easier said than done. But know one thing; I will never have these feelings about you. You have great energy!!

I love ♡ 🖤 🤍 you and wish you only bright light and easy tests.

Good morning ☼! Be in the present, for it is a present. Be passionate, have gratitude, be respectful, seek to understand, and always grow spiritually and intellectually. Know love and real happiness. Take care of your health. Last but not least, always choose your circle wisely, surround yourself with the best mastermind alliance, and always keep learning. This is my advice for life.

Decision Rule # 1: Keep a closed mouth and open eyes and ears. (I am working on this.)

Decision Rule #2: Opinions are the lowest and cheapest commodities. Keep your own counsel.

PS. . . I was so happy to spend time together downtown with you. Fun with the people you love is always a great thing. Let's promise to make the time to always enjoy and get together. Sending you tons of love ♡ 🖤 🤍.

Good afternoon ☼! I hope you're gearing up for the weekend! There are so many things that take place around us on any given day. Some seem mundane, some bring happiness, and some rub us the wrong way. Each is there to teach us a lesson. Things trigger us and our emotions constantly. The lesson is in how we respond—with anger or boredom?

Can we reverse those reactions to understanding and compassion or simply go to a neutral state versus anger or some robotic response?

The things that bring us happiness: Is it joy over someone's downfall or over gaining more money, or is it about seeing someone thrive, feeling gratitude, and being at peace? To evolve, identify the trigger and look for a new response; a small change can lead to bigger changes and evolution. My response to you is always love ♡🖤🩶 and gratitude, but I promise I am working on the nagging and exasperating responses, too!

Good morning ☼! I hope your morning is going smoothly! Thinking of you with love and admiration. When you were younger, it was about watching you grow physically.

Now I get to watch you move from strength to strength, growing in your craft and growing emotionally, intellectually, and spiritually. The key is to learn something from every experience, good or bad, and to be open to learning new things. The world has much to offer, and those who gain knowledge, information, and wisdom are at the top.

> *"Lessons are repeated until they are learned. A lesson will be presented to you in various forms until you have learned it. When you have learned it, you can go on to the next lesson. Learning lessons does not end. There's no part of life that doesn't contain its lessons. If you're alive, that means there are still lessons to be learned."*
> **—Cherie Carter-Scott**

The day you think you know everything is the day you know nothing. I love ♡🖤🩶 that you know something!

Good morning ☼! I hope you had a wonderful weekend! I think the reason people love dressing up during Halloween and putting on a costume, makeup, and changing their appearance is because it is liberating and fun. Being something other or maybe being what you really want to be. Think about it: Dressing up, and playing was something you could do nonstop when you were a kid but not so much as an adult.

Kids have magic inside them, and then society grinds it out. We all still have that magic inside of us. We just don't remember it.

We are part of a big universe filled with light and energy. People will not need to dress up or pretend when they tap into this field for themselves. This is enlightenment.

According to **Thich Nhat Hanh,**

> *"Enlightenment is when a wave realizes it is the ocean."*

You are the ocean; believe it. My love ♡🖤🍃 for you is as vast as any ocean.

Good morning ☼. I apologize for not messaging. I have to say; I fell into the trap of the cell phone. It took me many hours to upgrade, and while I'm glad I did, I miss my old phone; it seemed bigger, and I just felt way quicker on it. It felt sturdier too. I think that's what happens when you get used to something. You just figure, *this works, why change*? It's a fear of the unknown—trying new things. We don't even think, *hey, I'll get used to the new thing, too*. I admire the early adopters in the product life cycle.

One of the other problems is that newness costs more, so that is another reason we hold back. But at the end of the day, keep moving forward into the unknown. As per **Captain Kirk:**

> *"To explore strange new worlds, to seek out new life and new civilizations, to boldly go where no man has gone before."*

Be you and go for it always!

I love ♡🖤🍃 you to the next galaxy of change and beyond. Have a blessed day!

Good morning ☼**, and good afternoon!** Another week has flown by! I will always have your back and will always be a source to bring you positivity and supernova levels of energy. The word SELFLESS has the following definition:

> *"Concerned more with the needs and wishes of others than with one's own worth."*

However, if you look at the word, it also means I am less. Self-Less. I deserve less.

The word *selfish* has a negative meaning. However, I truly believe you have to take care of yourself first and put your needs first before you can take care of anyone else. You have to nurture yourself, or you will burn out doing for others.

If you do not take care of yourself and put yourself first, resentment and stress take control, which leads to sickness and disease. Dis-Ease

Why do you think on airplanes, they instruct you to put your oxygen mask on first before helping anyone else? Even before the child next to you? Because what help can you give if you're passed out or not thinking clearly from lack of oxygen? It's the same concept as not taking care of you. So, I say take the word *selfish* and change it to *self-love* ♡🖤🤍.

Good morning ☼! Hope your morning is going smoothly! While engaging in my morning routine, I was thinking about how fear and fear of failure are such dominating things. Worthiness is tied to these feelings too. Failure at times is not a bad thing, nor are hard times a sign of unworthiness. It is through these things that we grow and become resilient.
The thing is to learn from everything that is thrown at us and become stronger. What about being prepared? What about being ready? The idea that things in our environment don't change is old school. The world is always changing and evolving, and so are you. While we do not know the future, and I do not believe in stressing today over future possible outcomes, I do believe you can do everything now to build your mind and your technique to protect that mind.

- Take excellent care of your health and fitness.

- Build yourself intellectually, build the best networks of quality masterminds, and surround yourself with these people.

- Recognize and distance yourself from those who do not consider your feelings or who have become one-way streets.

Then you will be prepared to face any challenge, evil, or enemy who may try to rock you.

> *"The art of war teaches us to rely not on the likelihood of the enemy not coming, but on our own readiness to receive him; not on the chance of his not attacking, but rather on the fact that we have made our position unassailable."* —**Sun Tzu**

I love ♡🖤🤍 you and believe in you very much!

Good morning ☼! To my North Star, I want to share more brilliance from **James Clear**. I hope you got a chance to read *Atomic Habits*:

"Strangely, life gets harder when you try to make it easy. Exercising might be hard, but never moving makes life harder. Uncomfortable conversations are hard, but avoiding every conflict is harder. Mastering your craft is hard, but having no skills is harder. Easy has a cost."

Don't take the easy way out!

"When choosing a new habit, many people seem to ask themselves, 'What can I do on my best days?' The trick is to ask, 'What can I stick to even on my worst days?' Start small. Master the art of showing up. Scale up when you have the time, energy, and interest."

I send you energy with love ♡🖤🤎 to keep moving forward.

Good morning ☼! Another new day and week to start fresh and another opportunity to go for it. The best line I heard recently was someone saying, "Actually, I can." It's the truth. We can if we have the right frame of mind.

I think comedic icon Lucille Ball nailed it: *"I have an everyday religion that works for me. Love yourself first and everything else falls into line. You really have to love yourself to get anything done in this world."*

One of my favorite shows growing up was *I Love Lucy*. I laughed every time I watched it and didn't appreciate her genius until I was much older. She was a huge success and had her own show in a time when women did not have seat at the table. That statement was made years ago, and she was once again way ahead of her time and the curve.

So, love yourself, not in an ego way, but in the way that you take care of yourself and build yourself.

"Success is liking yourself, liking what you do and liking how you do it." —**Maya Angelou**

I happen to love ♡🖤🤎 you, what you do, and how you do it.

Good morning ☼! I hope you are having a great start to the day. A friend of mine gave me this great recommendation and I thought to share it with you. She advised me to get into the habit of asking myself honestly, "Does this support the life I'm trying to create?" If not, release it.

It can apply to so many things: relationships/friendships, business, habits, daily choices, you name it. We have so many thoughts and things going on daily but before you waste time pondering a thought, an action, an opportunity or a relationship you need to ask yourself, "Does this serve me? Is this in alignment with who I am or what I want to create for myself?" Once you answer this fundamental question, you will lose the distractions, streamline, and focus.

I can promise you that you are a major part of the life I created for myself. I love you ♡🖤💚 and bless you.

Good morning ☼. When I was your age, we had the saying TGIF: Thank G-d It's Friday. I don't think it's a popular phrase anymore. But it really fits any decade.

I just want to tell you that you impress the hell out of me in the way you conduct yourself with knowledge, confidence, independence, and respect. I'm in awe. I am so impressed with your achievements to date and your ability to think, strategize, plan, and adapt so that no matter how coocoo for Cocoa Puffs this world is, I firmly believe that you will succeed.

This is the greatest joy and ultimate success for any parent. I love ♡🖤💚 that you have given this gift to me.

Good morning ☼! Here is a great question to ask yourself and ponder over the weekend: What's the one action that moves the needle more than 100 other actions? What's the one choice that renders 1000 other choices irrelevant?

Most things are not worth optimizing. Master the big moves and move quickly and peacefully through the other stuff. For me the big thing will always be my love ♡🖤💚 for you.

Good morning ☼! I hope you are having a great week so far.

Thought for the day is that the ending is not set in stone. Although you cannot go back in time to make a brand-new start, you can always start from now and make a brand-new ending.

This is the beauty of the life we are living now. We all have this capability. Always know that you always have the chance to change the conversation, change the path and chart a new direction.

I love ♡🖤🩶 and bless you on your journey and the choices you make along the way.

Good morning ☼! As I get closer to the process of publishing a book, I caught myself starting to doubt. I realized the trigger was the money going into this project and by extension updating my website because it is not in alignment with who I am now, and the book has to be part of the whole experience. I realized that it does not take much to ignite a whole loop of negative thinking and feelings.

The best thing is to stop the cycle, recognize it, breathe, and turn the fear and self-defeating thoughts and feelings off that live in the left side of the brain and replace them with higher level positive thoughts and feelings by activating the right side of the brain.

> *"Very often, the things that you are most afraid of,*
> *are the things you just really need to go for it."*
> **—Olivia Newton-John**

As I have been on a journey for several years and am learning and reinventing, I want you to know that I admire and love ♡🖤🩶 you because you are already far ahead of where I was at your age and maybe even now.

Good morning ☼! I receive a newsletter from **Robin Sharma** and thought to share his advice directly as this is the best message to send you today since it is the start of the year:

"You've been graced with 12 pristine months, fresh and available for you to shape into your highest destiny. I know—and trust—you'll apply your genius well, as the months ahead unfold.

I encourage you to take some time today to ask yourself the following five questions:

1. Who must I become to make 2024 legendary?

2. What one breathtaking new project will I bring into the world this new year?

3. What [and who] must I let go of from last year to make 2024 wow?

4. What major daily habit will I install to make the next twelve months my best yet?

5. What gifts and talents within me must I salute and cherish more often? (Self-respect is a giant performance multiplier.)

Yes. Last year was full of tumult and turbulence and global troubles. Having said this, rough seas make great sailors. And challenging times breed true heroes.

So dismiss all the fearmongering, decry all the negativity and delete all apathy and roll up your sleeves to get busy handcrafting a year of exceptional creativity, productivity, prosperity and service to society. You CAN do this. Your most heroic self seeks this." ♡🖤🤎

Good afternoon ☼! I am tired of overscheduling myself and just not really enjoying any of it. It's more like getting through lists of things to do. So today while I am doing stuff, because I still have not mastered the busyness problem, I'm trying to stay in the chill zone, and I hope you find this zone too. The chill zone can be as simple as staring out the window, daydreaming, meditating, praying or just doing something you enjoy for a bit.

It's important to enjoy something daily. We are just so wired into doing or getting through or making things happen that it just doesn't end. So those moments of self-care are important so that you don't burn out.

Tell me one thing you do daily that you take time for and really enjoy. Love you ♡🖤🤎!

Good afternoon ☼. As I clean out the apartment during the big painting process, I am finding all of your old jerseys and sports stuff. I am going to have to figure out where to store this stuff. Seeing these brought back memories of you growing up and really into the Knicks, Chicago Bulls, Lakers—when legends ruled the courts.

Then I read a quote by the legend himself, Michael Jordan, which was serendipity. You know we are all limitless beings, but we are even more so when we work as a team and build each other up. When we use our brains which is our best resource. Always keep learning and growing because life is a long game; strive to be a champion.

"Talent wins games, but teamwork and intelligence win championships." —Michael Jordan

You're my team and my champion. ♡🖤🩶

Good morning ☼!

"Conversations are the currency of human connection."
—Susan Scott

What does this mean? To me it means that conversations bring us connections. Bring us meaning. That is what makes us human.

When I was young, there was no tech, so you had to talk. There was the house phone, and we would talk on it for hours. There was TV, and people would sit together and watch it and then talk about what they saw. Cable started and people started watching more and probably talking less.

I am sure that at first when the phone, then TV and later cable came about, it was considered a distraction because it did break conversing by gluing people to a box, and phones eliminated the need to meet and talk in person. But people had conversations.

Now we don't have conversations. People do not have the skill set to converse. Between tech and the over management of kids' time (Yes, I was guilty of that. Hello, NYC living!) many people today do not possess the skill set to converse. Society is losing the ability to form a connection which results in disconnect, greater depression, addiction, and stress. Now we have AI and algorithms controlling the conversation.

I started doing these text conversations with you because the most important thing to me is being a human to you and reaching you where you are. This is our own currency, and it is invaluable. ♡🖤🩶

Good afternoon ☼! Whatever your journey is, whatever lights you up and you want to pursue, go for it. Life is about the road, and we are here to fulfill our mission and destiny. There will always be the naysayers. These can be your own saboteurs or people who try to talk you out of things for "your own good" or because they "care."

Actor **Michael Caine**, a highly successful actor, has a different POV. *"I have a policy to never listen to anyone explain why they cannot do*

something." I agree, but here are my tweaks and I hope it resonates: "I have a policy to never listen to anyone who says I cannot do something." Or better yet, "I have a policy to never listen to myself explain why I cannot do something."

Follow your passion and don't talk yourself out of doing, achieving, or living due to input or your own self talk. I know you will think things through. I believe in you and your abilities. This is a part of the vast universe of love ♡🖤💚 that I have for you.

Good afternoon ☼. My dear friend, Marcy Axelrod, who authored a book called *How We Choose to Show Up*. Her message is that every day we have a choice:

Do we "Just Show Up" improvising as we go, phoning in our intentions?

Do we "Truly Show Up" living decisive moments with intent?

OR

Are we "Barely There" struggling to show up at all?

Showing up is the invisible system all around us, connecting us to our society, situations, selves and each other. And it's a contact sport. It's how we lead whether working, parenting, coaching, playing, empowering one another or steering a global company.

I have great faith in you and your ability to show up. And know that I will always show up for you ♡🖤💚.

Good morning ☼! The weekend provides a great opportunity to rest and restore. It provides an opportunity for self-care so that we can recharge. It also provides the much-needed time for reassessment.

Reassessing is reflecting on the past week, reviewing the calls and conversations you had, business and personal decisions you made, meetings you had, any other choices you made to see where you could have either improved or learned something. If it was the right thing you did, then why was it right? Keep a journal of these decisions of what worked and did not. See patterns and adjust. Keep a playbook that updates every weekend as you reassess.

By doing this, you will be building incredible brain muscle and opening up more areas of your brain activity. But best of all, you will start to look at things from all sides, from multiple viewpoints and not just one dominant POV. You will be able to call on the best course of action for each situation because your brain will be more fluid.

> *"When one worldview dominates your thinking, you'll try to explain every problem you face through that worldview. Read widely and reassess continually and realize there are many answers."* **—James Clear**

I send you love ♡🖤🩶 and blessings all day, every day.

*   *   *

Reflection:
EMBRACING THE LIFELONG JOURNEY OF GROWTH

As I reflect on my growth and personal development journey, I realize how my thought processes have evolved and changed. Though challenging and uncertain, the pandemic catalyzed my most significant personal evolution. It forced me to slow down and look within, to face the uncomfortable truth that I had been neglecting myself for far too long.

I realized that we are never "finished." Life is a continuous process of learning, adapting, and evolving. Every challenge, every setback, has the potential to be a lesson that enriches our journey. This mindset, more than anything else, became my guiding light.

I wanted to pass this wisdom on to my sons: Growth isn't just about success or achievements; it's about being open to change, embracing discomfort, and understanding that setbacks don't define us. As I embraced personal development, I found my confidence growing, my sense of self-worth expanding, and my ability to navigate life's challenges with resilience. I wanted my sons to know that this journey never stops. When you think you've learned it all, that's the moment when growth slows down. But when you remain curious, humble, and eager to learn, life opens new opportunities, perspectives, and paths.

To my sons, I hope you always carry this with you: Personal growth is a lifelong commitment, one that requires patience, self-compassion, and an openness to change. It will not always be easy, but it will always be worth it. Never stop learning, never stop evolving, and never stop believing that you can always grow into the best version of yourself.

My wish is that you embrace growth as the journey to fulfillment. The journey of personal development is not about perfection but about progress. It's about learning to adapt, rising from challenges stronger than before, and continually shaping a life that aligns with your deepest values. Growth is not a destination but a lifelong journey, and it's never too late to begin.

CHAPTER 7

Love Relationships

Love is the reason I started sending daily messages to my kids. It is all about love, and everything begins and ends with it. No matter what age, every person wants to know that they were loved by their parents and that their parents thought highly of them. People yearn for this their whole lives. I was moved by the comments and messages I received after self-publishing *Text Messages to My Sons* first edition. Messages from people about how they wished their parents would tell them that they loved them. That someone had done this for them when they were growing up. Someone messaged me asking if I would be their mom. It broke my heart, to be honest.

When I was a kid, the kids who got those love notes from their parents in their lunch boxes seemed happy. I was envious because I did not receive any messages with my lunch. For me, the proof of the importance of sending love above all else and building relationships is the foreword that my sons wrote. If you have not read it, please do. They speak about the impact of knowing someone loves them enough to send a message to them daily. That someone cares enough to do it. Even though they "know" their mom loves them, they feel more energy with these messages. The truth is that when I die, they are not going to think about what I bought them when they were in high school or the money I spent; they are going to miss the messages. While I express my love in every message I send, I do not expect them to tell me they love me back; there is no conditionality about sending love. It is given by me with no strings attached. You must be willing to provide this for your child and not be exasperated because they do not answer your questions or respond how you want them to.

Today, with the rampant rise in hate, misinformation, indoctrination, propaganda, bullying, and violence online and continuously on social media, it is more important now than ever to message your kids love. It is also imperative to teach them that they are worthy and have high value no matter how many followers and likes they have. It is natural for young adults and teenagers to question themselves during their quest for independence. It is not a good idea for social media to define this for them. It is up to you.

⚬ ⚬ ⚬

Good morning ☼! I hope you had a good restorative sleep and an even better start to the day. Start the day knowing you are cherished, loved beyond reason, and respected. All you have to do on your end is to know this, be confident, be grateful, and take the feeling and radiate it out. If you keep this in mind, everything on the inside and outside will be glorious and in the flow. ♡♥🖤

> *"The moment you change your perception is the moment you rewrite the chemistry in your body."* —**Dr. Bruce Lipton**

Good morning ☼! It's another weekend coming up! One thing is for sure; it does not matter how many weeks, months, or years go by; my love and wishes for you are endless. I send you blessings for good health, happiness, positivity, and abundance in all things. Be happy and make this your mantra:

"Day by day, in every way, I am getting better and better."
—Émile Coué

I'm so happy I did something right in that my kids are close to each other and such wonderful siblings. ♡🖤🩶

Good morning ☼! I hope you had a great weekend! I am so excited that we will be leaving for a family vacation in less than 1 week! I realize how many times I personally missed the opportunity to take these precious family trips. I chose to work during this time versus spending time with you. For many years I did this. I can say now that it was a mistake. To be able to be with you without responsibilities and just relax and enjoy is priceless.

In reality, we move in different directions; we have obligations and responsibilities that get in the way of being together. Life is a busy thing. But I'm glad we are choosing this time, this year, whether it is one week, or 2 weeks, to be together and enjoy.

I love ♡🖤🩶 you dearly and look forward to a beautiful, restorative, and bonding trip together. Life is about making great memories with the ones you love!

Good morning ☼! Today I was a guest on a podcast, and the host asked me the following question, "What does being a mom mean to you?" Honestly, it's everything. It's what gets me up each morning and the most important thing in life. I love ♡🖤🩶 you that much.

Good afternoon ☼! Happy April Fool's Day! This is not an April Fool's message! I don't fool around when I'm sending you love ♡🖤🩶 and blessings. It's for real. The real deal!

Good morning ☼! Do you know what is so special about the time frame of August–October? Some people would say:

1. Good weather

2. Long holiday weekend

3. The High Holiday cycle

4. Fall partying/Halloween

5. Football/baseball

6. Vacation time

You get what I mean! But to me, it is the best time of year because this was when I gave birth to:

1. The 3 best happenings in my life

2. The 3 best creations in existence

3. The 3 biggest, most extraordinary miracles to ever happen to me

4. The 3 best reasons to get up every day and keep going

5. The 3 best sons in the world

My list goes forever ♡🖤🤍.

Good morning ☼! I love you so much! Today is Grandma's birthday, and as I was thinking about her and remembering her, this message came directly to me. It is a WOW that it showed up at the precise moment when I needed to see it. It is a reminder that those we love ♡🖤🤍 may physically be gone, but their soul is somewhere close.

> *"Those we love don't go away. They walk beside us every day, unseen, unheard, but always near, still loved, still missed, and very dear."* **—Alex MacLean**

Good morning ☼! While another week has gone by, these past few days have been a bit different because the apartment is quiet and very clean. But even with those benefits, I miss having all 3 of you under 1 roof, under my roof. I really enjoyed these past 4 months together.

Being with you guys brings me warmth, happiness, and contentment. I also find your conversations to be next level.

I appreciated every moment of having you all home, and I just wanted you to know this. I love ♡🖤🩶 you and send you the highest level of energy and light.

Good morning ☼! I realize since you are all living at home again, you may find it is not necessary for me to send my messages. But the truth is that sending a message of inspiration and love and sharing knowledge is not dependent on location. True, when I don't physically see you, I have a greater drive to message. But I find the thoughts, words, and emotions I put into these messages are something special, and it is important to do. It really has nothing to do with physical proximity. Message the people you care about, to give them love, support, knowledge, and inspiration because not only will you make their day better, but you will make your day better. I guarantee this because telling you I love ♡🖤🩶 you makes my day better.

Good morning ☼! Thinking of you and hoping you are having a good start to the week and feeling great both in body and mind. Thinking about me too, and I am hoping one day you will send me or, hopefully, your kids' messages, too. Sending you love ♡🖤🩶 and blessings always, every day, every minute.

Good morning ☼! As I get older, I realize family is the most important thing. Enriching our relationship and being part of and involved in each other's life is the priority. Family really is at the top of the goal pyramid, followed by health & fitness, business, career, character, intellect, spiritual development, and social connections. Family is the touchstone, and while sometimes families may cause hurt and certain dysfunction, there still is that unconditional love, deep bond, and protection that is unique amongst family members. You are my family, and I love ♡🖤🩶 you the most! Don't ever forget it.

Good morning ☼! Here we are at hump day—although since Monday was a holiday, it kind of makes sense that Wednesday really came quickly. Now that we are all back living together due to leases being up and college graduation, it's a good idea to examine what this means. The

5 of us have not been living at home under one roof since 2012. There were a few summers that you were all home at the same time—was it 2017 or 2018? I think it's important we all respect each other's feelings and understand that while you may feel inconvenienced or unsettled, we do too. It's important we don't stay frustrated or impatient but just go with the flow and know there are no bad intentions. Respect requests and boundaries. Also, take the time to be still and breathe because that will help clear out any negativity and get your head on track. Go out for walks! I think this quote from **Hermann Hesse**, author of the classic *Utopia*, was written about living with your parents:

> **"Within you, there is stillness and a sanctuary to which you can retreat at any time and be yourself."**

I personally will cherish this gift of more time with you because I know it is just that, a gift. I love ♡❤🤍 you and will do my best to not get on your nerves! No promises, though!!

Good afternoon ☼! Jet lag and just getting back into the swing of things after being away for the last 2 weeks. I can only say that I had the best time being with you in Morocco and Israel. It really fills me up to be able to share experiences and spend time together in a different environment, different culture, celebrating family and life. It means so much to have experiences, to create memories together, and carve out moments because, let's face it, life is about creating moments that become wonderful memories. As time goes by, this is what we reflect on. We reflect on past experiences that stand out in our memories. That's what brings us joy, comfort, strength, or despair and pain. My goal is to create memories with you that bring the best emotions. I know it is not always possible or realistic, but it's a worthy pursuit.

Being with you brings me a feeling I cannot explain. It just fills my soul. I love ♡❤🤍 you so deeply that words can never truly capture the feeling.

Good morning ☼! When you can't make it to Friday night dinner, I'm sad because I miss seeing you, but when I can't make it, I feel worse! But I figured you can put the picture of your father and I that I just sent to your phone on your table, so you know we are energetically with you! I love ♡❤🤍 you and will send down a good assortment of food tonight!

Good morning ☼! The best part of the High Holidays was spending time with you! Just being in your company makes me extraordinarily happy. It's not even anything you say or do, just being around you. I love ♡🖤🤍 you so much—it amazes me sometimes the depth of my feelings. You are a one and only, a unique creation in this universe.

Good morning ☼! My first thought this morning, on the way to the airport, was that I must get my message of love, power, peace, and abundance to you. I really prefer to send it earlier versus later. Why? Because there is nothing like starting the day knowing you are massively loved ♡🖤🤍, that there is immense gratitude knowing that you are in the world and that the world is yours to achieve whatever you dream. No limits.

Good morning ☼! It is a very special day today. It's Grandma's birthday, and she would have been 80! I know she is in a good place, and what we are left with are the memories and her funny statements to sustain us. She was the epitome of cool, fashion, and fire. Pushing forward and always moving—going forward was what Grandma was about. She was a modern thinker and could smell BS a mile away. She always believed in you and knew you would succeed; she knew you were the best. Know this always. She loved ♡🖤🤍 you deeply.

Good morning ☼! I can't wait until the end of the message to say I love you today, tomorrow, and until the end of time. I am sending you the highest frequency and best energy to last not just today but through the weekend. You are my hero, and I am super proud of you. You impress me daily. I think this is all I want to say and not dilute the power of this message with insights and quotes like usual. That's all great stuff, but I will get back to it on Monday. You are my world ♡🖤🤍.

Good morning ☼! I was thinking about the impact of friendships and the importance of your social group. It can really go either way with peers. How you feel about yourself is what you will attract, but there are many factors that determine who you hang out and spend time with.

*"I argue that the most powerful thing you can do to add
healthy years is to curate your immediate social network.
In general, you want friends with whom you can have a
meaningful conversation. You can call them on a bad day,
and they will care. Your group of friends is better than
any drug or anti-aging supplement and will do more for
you than just about anything."* —**Dan Buettner**

I adore ♡🖤🩶 you and feel fortunate that you have wonderful friends and a great social network.

Good morning ☼! How is it we are at another Friday? What is going on here? As time plows on, I can say for certain that I love watching you grow, evolve, and keep moving forward. I continually see new facets of you appearing, ways of thinking, and doing. You are always growing and building, and it awes me! Listening to you speak and have conversations blows my mind because I realize not only how advanced you are but how you are light years ahead of where I was at your age!

Keep doing you, and there will never be any limits! I love ♡🖤🩶, adore, respect, and admire you!

*"Thank the old you for helping you to evolve into the
newer and more badass version of yourself."* —**Unknown**

Good morning ☼! Can you believe another weekend is here? Time goes forward whether we want it to or not. This is why we must always be present and take the time to say I love ♡🖤🩶 you; I am proud of you; I respect you, and I appreciate you. You are one in a multiple of trillions; I wish the best for you, more than the best, actually. I am the luckiest and most prideful person and mom to have you as my son.

There is always a seat for you at my table, and remember, when it comes to any other table that you want to sit at,

*"If they don't give you a seat at the table, bring a
folding chair."* —**Shirley Chisholm**

Good morning ☼! I just wanted to say how truly wonderful it was to be together with extended family for Thanksgiving. I really enjoyed the experience and hope it becomes a tradition! Best of all is driving around with the 3 of you in the backseat. All we needed was a Power Rangers video, and it will feel like back in the day! I love ♡🖤🩶 you, and spending time together tops my wish list every time!

Good morning ☼. Another Monday. Busy week coming up, so I hope you had a restful and restorative weekend. I am going to keep this short and sweet. You are the sunshine of my life—yes, that is a song—but that is what you are. You are my light. I love ♡🖤🩶 you; there is no quantity or amount that can describe how much. Be you and be great because you are this and more.

Good morning ☼! I hope you had fun over the weekend and got a chance to rest. I was so thrilled to be together with family to celebrate! We should always make the time to celebrate life more often as it is a good life and worth acknowledging! I realize family and connections are so foundational to our existence. True, family can also bring you down at times, but blood is thicker than water, and most families will always have your back! Here's to family! I'm so glad you are mine! ♡🖤🩶

Good morning ☼! Each day brings me another opportunity to start my day by letting you know how much I love you—it's my most favorite morning ritual. Nothing starts my day better than blessing you and sending my love. It's a daily action that has become part of my thought process. My love ♡🖤🩶 and feelings for you are in my actions, thoughts, body, and soul. It just flows continuously, with no break, no starts and stops, no beginning or end.

Good morning ☼! Another year of high holidays has ended. I appreciate every minute you were able to spend with us. Yes, it is an incredibly special and meaningful time of year, but for me, what makes it the most special to me is seeing you, your spirituality, your respect for traditions and heritage, and your generosity and support. It warms me and makes me very proud. I love ♡🖤🩶 you, and I know I am very blessed to be your mom.

Good morning ☼! I had a great time last night and I am glad we were all together to celebrate your father's birthday!

Far too many times, one of you was always somewhere in the world, but this time we were all together and I really love that. Listening to you laugh and talk with adults that you have known since you were little is a sight to behold. You know how to hold your own, connect, and engage. You make me a proud mom! I love ♡🖤🩶 and admire you!

Good morning ☼! This was a great weekend for me because I had all three of my sons over for Friday night dinner and a good part of the day on Saturday. As I get older, I am grateful for my family and friends. Yes, family connotes a blood bond, but it does not have to be by blood. Family are those people who you have familiarity with, who bring comfort, who share your ups and downs, who stand the test of time and who have been woven into the fabric of your life. It is true that family can be stabilizing or destabilizing, and one has to be grateful to have familial ties that make them stronger. Know you are loved and that there are people who truly care about you, like I do. Anyone is family to me that love ♡🖤🩶 you.

Good morning ☼! Rolling into another weekend!

I received a lovely message this morning from a friend in India.

JUDGE nothing. . . . *You will be HAPPY . . .*

FORGIVE everything . . . *You will be HAPPIER . . .*

LOVE everything . . . *You will be HAPPIEST . . .*

I thought it was short (which you love), sweet (which everyone loves) and meaningful (which I love).

But most of all, I love ♡🖤🩶 everything about you, and it is enough for me!

Good morning ☼! Happy Monday! I hope you had a wonderful weekend.

I have to say I really enjoyed the weekend, staying at the beach with your father. What is great is that I did what I love to do, and he did what he loves to do, and we also did things together. But the point is, and it is a good one, is that in a relationship you can be your own person and do you but also come together, come back to each other, and do "couple" things. It is healthy to take care of and serve yourself; bring happiness to yourself, do things that enrich your soul, then you can be a better partner and person.

Please know that I never minded putting you first because you are everything good and amazing in my life and I love ♡🖤🩶 you and your brothers exponentially. But in life I realize I might have been a better mom had I practiced more self-care.

Good afternoon ☼! We have a lot to be grateful for even if the world seems upside down and twisted.

Friendship is one of those things, and I am grateful that you have amazing friends who are good people. You have surrounded yourself with peers who are worthy of you, friends that allow you to grow and be you, without competitiveness, judgment, or jealousy. Your friends admire and love you. And if there is someone in your group who does not embody the above, keep your distance.

Here is a quote from author and poet **Maya Angelou** on finding your family:

> *"Family isn't always blood. It's the people in your life who want you in theirs; the ones who accept you for who you are. The ones who would do anything to see you smile and who love you no matter what."*

I may be your mom and your family, but I hope you feel that I accept you for who you are too. I always want more for you, but I love ♡🖤🩶 the human being you are.

Good morning ☼. Time is always moving but the one thing that can be a constant is the relationships we build and maintain and the friendships we make.

True, we sometimes just have people in our lives who become close friends for a certain timeframe. They come into our life to teach us or help us through or to open our eyes about something; many times you both move on after. At the end of the day, friendship and relationships are the secret sauce of life.

I admire that you have built a network of amazing friends who love ♡🖤🤍 you and that you are also smart enough to see each person for who they are. Anyone who claims you as a friend is very lucky indeed. I am blessed knowing you have a beautiful circle around you.

Good afternoon ☼! I was thinking about how important your tribe is, the people who you surround yourself with. When you are born and growing up, you have little choice on what tribe you live with. In essence you are totally dependent on everything from your tribe. You subconsciously learn and do everything to fit in with the tribe, so you are not exiled.

Some tribes are horrible, and some are great. It really has an impact on how you grow, see yourself, and how you handle life. This affects everything.

But then there comes a point where you start choosing who you want to surround yourself and align with. You start mapping consciously and subconsciously who your tribe is. Your original tribe is still there, but you get to create your own.

I'm so grateful that you have always chosen wisely. Surrounding yourself with friends, colleagues, and mentors who elevate you, believe in you, and care about you. This is a gift. I am always going to be in your tribe no matter what. You are the best tribe I have ever had. ♡🖤🤍

* * *

Reflection: THE ENDURING POWER OF LOVE

As I reflect on the power of love and relationships, I am filled with a deep sense of peace and purpose. Love truly is the foundation of everything. It is the fuel that propels us, the glue that binds us, and the light that guides us through life. The simple act of sending a text message each day is my way of reminding my sons that they are loved and valued no matter what life throws their way.

When I first began this practice, it was about more than just expressing my love. It was about giving them a constant reminder that no matter how old they got, no matter how independent they became, my love for them would always be unwavering and unconditional. And as I watched them grow into young men, I realized just how important those messages have been for them and me. The love I send isn't just for their benefit; it fills my heart with warmth, knowing that I am leaving behind something lasting that they can hold onto forever.

The world is a different place now than when I was growing up. With the rise of technology, social media, and constant connectivity, the world's noise can sometimes drown out the simple yet powerful message of love. In this age of distraction, it is more crucial than ever to remind our children that they are enough, just as they are, and that they are loved unconditionally, not for what they achieve or how many likes and followers they get, but for who they are at their core.

To my sons, I hope you always feel the depth of my love in every message, every word. I hope you carry this love with you, not just from me but all the people who cherish you. Know that you are never alone, never forgotten, and always loved—no matter where life takes you.

My wish is that you remember the profound impact that love and connection can have. It's easy to get caught up in the hustle of life, but the most important thing we can give to our children, loved ones, and ourselves is love—not conditional, not transactional, but pure, unconditional love. Let that love be a daily reminder of your worth and value and the deep connections that sustain us all.

In the end, love will be remembered. It will echo long after we're gone. So, send your love often, with no expectations or strings attached, and watch as it transforms your relationship, your family, and your world.

CHAPTER 8

Time
Nature

Time is a manufactured concept. We know so little about it. Everything seems to be linear. You progress through life, and it moves forward. But does it? I was surprised at how much the past affects our present and future. I was learning about being present and that it truly is a present. I wanted to share with my kids to be more present and notice what is around them. I shared that every minute, hour, day, week, month, and year is an opportunity to start something new. I tried to explain how the past can affect you as a saboteur or friend in the present and future. This is why it was vital for me to be accountable to them for my actions because it is devastating to think that my actions could have caused trauma or doubt to my kids. I also wanted them to understand that the future is undetermined, so not to worry about it.

I wanted my kids to understand that time cannot be regained once it passes. I wanted them to slow down and appreciate life and prioritize what truly matters in life.

Time and nature provide balance and harmony. I remember

growing up with a backyard and kids on my block. We played outside all day and made up games and things to do. We built stuff, and we were very aware of and tuned into nature.

I raised my sons in Manhattan, the concrete jungle. I over managed, putting them into too many activities and exceptionally long days at school in a dual curriculum education. I was fortunate that, for the most part, the explosion of social media and algorithms was not as intense as it is now, but they spent plenty of time in front of a screen. However, their happiest and best times were at sleepaway camp. It was apparent why: the fresh air, trees, space, and freedom to run and play and be boys was just heaven.

With the rise in technology and screen usage, kids are not as outdoors as they used to be.

I realize now that nature is restorative for the mind. My kids are grown; they are adults, and I started sharing messages about nature, breathing, and getting closer to trees, water, and air to remind them that they need to incorporate breaks from the concrete jungle where we still live. I believe G-d creates all things, and acknowledging nature is my way of connecting my kids to something larger than themselves and seeing beauty.

❀ ❁

Good morning ☼! As I wait for my connecting flight in Denver for NYC, I realize I will be exchanging mountains for skyscrapers. I was thinking about the difference between using imagination versus having the real experience to draw on, of being somewhere and feeling the breeze, smelling the air, listening to the sounds, and having live images in your mind to draw upon. I know now that when I am home and taking breaks to refresh my mind, instead of thinking about abstract thoughts or what's on my task list, I will look at the pictures on my phone and in my head from Utah, close my eyes, feel the wind, recall the scents and sounds. I will practice being still. I will slow down and simply be. I will remember those mountains and breathe. Sending you mountains and mountains of love ♡♥♥, peace, serenity, and abundance.

Good morning ☀️! I hope your weekend was restorative. You can really feel the change coming from winter to spring; I think the spring solstice was yesterday, so we are officially in spring. Just the name *spring* means vaulting forward into new beginnings and life cycle renewals. I look at my plants, and I'm telling you they are aware spring has begun. So, in honor of this opportunity to refresh and welcome new beginnings, I thought this quote is good advice to improve our garden so that we may flourish:

> *"We plant seeds that will flower as results in our lives,*
> *so best to remove the weeds of anger, avarice, envy,*
> *and doubt." —Dorothy Day*

You're the best thing I ever planted! I love ♡🖤💚 you and love watching you flourish.

Good morning ☀️! I hope your day is starting off beautifully, full of gratitude, great energy, and health! As always, my first thought of the day is about sending you lots of love ♡🖤💚. There is a lot to be said about water. The earth is covered in it; there is way more water than land; our bodies have a big percentage of water; we simply cannot live without it. Water is creation and gives life. Water can also easily destroy. The water is affected by the tides. The rough seas and shifting tides affect human beings' moods. With this being said, I wanted to share about Dr. Masaru Emoto's Water Experiment Proof, "The Mind Can Affect the Physical."

What has put Dr. Emoto at the forefront of the study of water is his proof that thoughts and feelings affect physical reality. By producing different focused intentions through written and spoken words and music and literally presenting it to the same water samples, the water appears to "change its expression."

Dr. Emoto discovered that crystals formed in frozen water reveal changes when specific, concentrated thoughts are directed toward them. He found that water from clear springs and water that has been exposed to loving words shows brilliant, complex, and colorful snowflake pattern crystallizations. In contrast, polluted water, or water exposed to negative thoughts, forms incomplete, asymmetrical patterns with dull colors.

The implications of this research create a new awareness of how we can positively impact the earth and our personal health.

Good morning ☼! Another beautiful day. I don't mind cool weather—it brings fresh air, and it really wakes up the brain cells!

When the sun is out with fresh, cool air, for me, it is not only refreshing, but I see potential and opportunities because my brain is getting recharged. So, I recommend, on days like this, going out and walking. Schedule a break and go out. Don't grab lunch or do errands—just walk and breathe. Not only will your brain thank you because you gave it air and a break, but it will reward you with even better performance when you go back to your job or whatever task you need to do. Who knows, it may lead to thinking up the next great thing or getting started on something new! Sending you tons of sunshine and fresh air mixed with lots of love ♡🖤🩶 and blessings!

Good morning ☼! I am looking at my windowsill garden, which also means that I am looking outside the window. I'm wondering if my orchids will re-bloom. They keep getting new leaves on the bottom, but the orchid has not re-bloomed. But I figure they will re-bloom when the time is right. Orchids are interesting because you never know when they will come back. My other plants are thriving. Orchids mimic life. They have all this beauty, and even when the flower falls off, there is this potential to re-bloom and be beautiful again. Even after just looking like a stick, more or less with a few green leaves on the very bottom, one day, they just become gorgeous again. Wouldn't it be great if they just stayed in bloom all the time? Would we appreciate their beauty less? I think it's the opposite with people. We should strive to be happy and in bloom both internally and externally, not just in cycles. I say downtime and growth are for during the sleep cycle! While you are awake—be blooming and in your glory. According to **Mahatma Gandhi**:

> *"Happiness is when what you think, what you say, and
> what you do are in harmony."*

These things together keep you blooming! I love ♡🖤🩶 you to the bloom and beyond!

Good afternoon ☼! How is your day going? I'm still thinking about time. It seems to be a theme or just something I'm noticing a lot. When you are ready to receive, G-d sends the messages directly to you. So, today and tomorrow, I am going to share some time-related messages.

> *"Six months from now, you will have either 6 months*
> *of excuses or 6 months of progress—you choose."*
> **—Unknown**

This is interesting to me because I remember when I started my MBA, working full time and going at night. I thought, "Wow, this will take me about 5 years." This seemed like a long commitment at the time. But when I really thought about it, I realized that I could spend the time going out to great restaurants and clubs, partying, traveling, and hanging out with friends, or I could spend a lot less time doing those things and get an MBA. The 5 years flew by; I got an MBA, got married, and had my first baby born 16 months after graduating. It all flowed!

Use your time wisely:

> *"Balance peak intensity, focus, and productivity to*
> *achieve your goals with cycles of genuine recovery."*
> **—Robin Sharma**

This is the secret to great success, happiness, and longevity. I love ♡♥🖤 your tons.

Good morning ☼! Can you believe it? Another Friday, and just like that, we hurl into a new month. I feel like I constantly repeat this "Can you believe it's Friday" message, but it's the real deal. Fridays continually come, and as you get older, they come faster. As **Robert Frost** says:

> *"In three words, I can sum up everything I've learned about*
> *life. It goes on."*

Time and life go on. I hope peace goes on. One thing I know unequivocally is that my love ♡♥🖤 for you will go on whether I'm on this earth or not.

Good morning ☼! OMG, another Friday, the last one of January. It seems like time is going even faster. This brings me back to my previous message theme about our time and focus. Where are we spending our time? Are we spending it where it best serves us to build and achieve positive out-comes? Are we overly distracted, which takes from our cognitive ability?

> *"You do something all day long, don't you? Everyone*
> *does. If you get up at seven o'clock and go to bed at*
> *eleven o'clock, you have put in sixteen good hours, and*
> *it's certain with most people that they have been doing*
> *something all the time. They have been walking, reading,*
> *writing, or thinking. The only trouble is they do it about a*
> *great many things, and I do it about one. If they took the*
> *time in question and applied it in one direction, to one*
> *object, they would succeed."* —Thomas Edison

Wow, this quote hits it on the head. So, here's to great focus, which leads to great success! I love ♡🖤🤍 you regardless of your focus.

I wish you a blessed weekend and simply adore you!

Good morning ☼! I had a lovely walk in Central Park today with a close friend. It was just wonderful being in the company of a good person and walking along a path lined with trees and greenery.

Both of our middle names are JOY, and I thought we are light, joy bringers in this moment in time. But one should try to spread joy as often as possible. Wouldn't that make for a better world?

You are my light, my joy bringer, and I love ♡🖤🤍 you!

Good morning ☼! I was thinking this morning about the word *son* be-cause it sounds exactly like the word *sun*. I also realized I was organically starting my messages with either "Good morning (sunshine)" or when I'm running later, "Good afternoon (sunshine)". I think this was intuitive, add-ing the image of the sun to my messages to you.

My mind was automatically connecting son and sun. I know this to be true because you are the light of my light. The light I look to that has always brightened some dark places in my mind and life. This light is what has always kept me going and made me stronger. It gives me great comfort and meaning. I am evolving because of your light, which I have embodied. I love ♡🖤🤍 you totally and completely. Have a bright and beautiful day!!

Good afternoon ☼! Today is my last day of hiking in Utah. And once again, a completely different hiking experience. It was like being an explorer going through narrow passageways, narrow openings. Literally stepping sideways on small ledges to get up and seriously going on my butt to get down.

I even used my hands frequently to grab onto rocks while climbing up. It's extraordinary to see the impact of nature and the elements over millions of years. Sandstorms, water, lava, and continental shifts have created this landscape that is home to many types of formations, plants, and secrets. It's a miracle.

We walked through the valley today. I knew G-d was with me. I looked at the bluest sky and thought about my experience and thought I am blessed.

Thinking of my blessings always brings me to thoughts of you. I love ♡♥♥ and treasure you! You, too, are one of life's miracles.

Good morning ☼! I am sitting in my meditation room and staring, as usual, at my plants. Thinking how nice it is to see blue skies and sun even if the temperature outside is cold. I then started thinking about how the plants must feel when there is sunlight versus dark clouds, gray skies, or night. I talk to them in the morning and touch them. I pray in the morning near them and bless you while speaking to them. I feel they hear me, and it's comforting to them.

They are green and growing, so something is making them happy. I was also thinking about the trees; they are sentinels, witnesses to many things.

These sentinels provide oxygen; they provide shelter, they provide food; we need them for life. I was thinking how unbelievable all this creation is and how G-d made it with a thought. G-d keeps creating, and I believe that I am thinking about nature, the plants, earth, and trees because G-d wants me to know I'm on the right track. That all G-d's creations are alive, they function, have purpose, listen, and feel. They have something to tell us if we listen.

Sending you tons of love ♡♥♥ and sharing wisdom from above!

Good morning ☼! Friday! Thank G-d it's Friday. I will probably revisit the time theme at some point because it's such a big, vast topic. What does it mean?

It is definitely a man-made concept. Does it really exist? What about parallel universes and dimensions?

Oh boy—going out there! Here is a great thing to reflect on; if each day you look at your routine and pick either a new habit to start or invest time to make just small daily improvements to those habits, consistently over time it will not only lead to amazing results but change the trajectory of your life.

You change the trajectory of my life regularly in a great way. Every habit I work to improve on is with you in mind so I can be a good role model. I love ♡🖤🦓 you, and loving you is the best habit I have.

Good afternoon ☼! Today, I hiked at Zion Park! I challenged myself by hiking the hardest trail—Angels Landing. We got to the top. I had to stop and rest, breathing hard, but I did it! I was in awe of the mountains, trees, and streams, just admiring the overwhelming beauty. I was thinking of how lucky I am to be here, to have this life, and to have you in my life. I practiced stillness in these mountains, and it was an unbelievable experience. I realize it is hard for me to be still and present and take in the everyday wonder. Being still is incredible.

I love ♡🖤🦓 you; you are part of my soul! Please consider a hiking trip in the future!

Good morning ☼! I'm sitting on a bench near Central Park. It is so beautiful, especially with the weather warming up. Sitting here, I started reading and saw a quote that struck me. It has probably been around for a while, but for some reason, I am just noticing it now and want to share it because it is seriously great advice:

"I broke up with my fears to marry my dreams." **—Unknown**

That's a wow, no matter what context. Don't let fear stop you from going for it and living your life vision. I love ♡🖤🦓 you across the galaxies.

Good morning ☼! Wow today is a glorious NYC summer day. It might even be a top ten; breeze, low humidity, and sun. Precious days because these top ten days are countable during the year. We appreciate these really good weather days because they are rare. That's life—the polarities of good and the challenging. Polarity is yin and yang, the balance. We are lucky if we have balance. Learn from the challenges and capitalize on the good. Challenging is not bad; it's just another type of opportunity; view it this way, and you will always be grateful, and your life will be good. There is no polarity when it comes to my love ♡🖤🧡 for you!

Good morning ☼! I thought I'd share this beautiful reflection from Buddhist monk **Thich Nhat Hanh** on life:

> *"When you are a young person, you are like a young*
> *creek, and you meet many rocks, many obstacles,*
> *and difficulties on your way. You hurry to get past these*
> *obstacles and get to the ocean. But as the creek moves*
> *down through the fields, it becomes larger and calmer,*
> *and it can enjoy the reflection of the sky. It's wonderful.*
> *You will arrive at the sea anyway, so enjoy the journey.*
> *Enjoy the sunshine, the sunset, the moon, the birds,*
> *the trees, and the many beauties along the way.*
> *Taste every moment of your daily life."*

Remember to feel my love ♡🖤🧡 every moment in the here and now. Sending you blessings and have a superlative weekend.

Good morning ☼! It is another Friday. Where is the time going? I will tell you that it's moving forward, and the future is not written. This quote from **Steve Jobs** is very relevant about connecting the dots:

> *"You can't connect the dots looking forward; you can*
> *only connect them looking backward. So, you have to*
> *trust the dots will somehow connect in your future.*
> *You have to trust in something—your gut, destiny, life,*
> *karma, whatever. This approach has never let me down,*
> *and it has made all the difference in my life."*

Everything you come across, learn, and experience is there to serve you in the future if you take the time to realize it. The worst things and best things, the lows and the highs, serve you. Do not accept any labels assigned to you; no one defines you. G-d created you perfectly. Think of yourself only by putting positive images in your mind and repeat positive statements in the present tense; I am . . . I think of you with abundant love ♡🖤🤍 and blessings always.

Good morning ☼! Another day, another week, what is time really any-way? It's a way humans mark things. Beginning, middle, and end. It moves on; we count things; numbers, minutes, hours, days, weeks, months, years. We live by the clock and the calendar.

We set alarms; we make lists and future plans. So interesting, but does it exist, or is it merely a construct? In other words, are we living through many times simultaneously—just not aware of it?

I don't know. The best advice: Live in the moment. Not in any other time. Don't get stuck in the past or worry and rush to the future. Just be in the now and make the most of now. Notice the wonder and the awe of everything around you. Then you will really live, and your mind will expand. ♡🖤🤍

Good morning ☼! It's a rainy Thursday, but that's okay because we need rain to make the bloom. The bloom of flowers brings joy and beauty to the world, and the bloom also brings pollination and the growth of our natural food products. Rain is very important, not to mention water means survival! It takes a lot of action for the rain to be created and fall, for the flowers to bloom, for the plants to grow, to water the fields and collect the water and bring it to our homes, businesses, etc. Action makes not just singular things happen but a chain of things happen. Each action brings another one after it.

Could you imagine if the power behind all this action just stopped and said, "I don't feel like it," or "I can't handle doing this, or "It's too much?" What would happen and be the result? Chaos! Mad Max in real life. A ton of fear! **Norman Vincent Peale** said:

> *"Action is a great restorer and builder of confidence.*
> *Inaction is not only the result but the cause of fear."*

Keep moving forward. Motivation comes after the first actionable step, not before, and keeps you moving. Inaction paralyzes. I love ♡🖤🩶 you and enjoy watching the steps you take!

Good morning ☼! This is the first hump day (Wednesday) of the new year. Guess what? There will be another 51 of them through the end of the year. It's interesting when you put it into perspective. We take it for granted in a lot of ways that there will always be another one of something. But really what we do each day affects the next one, so always try to do your best and if it's not the best day, then learn from it so the next one is better. Because life is a sequence of days and there may always be many, many of them.

Every day is an opportunity for love to grow and that is the best part. I love ♡🖤🩶 you endlessly.

Good morning ☼! I have deep gratitude for rain. Water is life, yet many people find it an inconvenience. I'm not sure where they think the water from the faucet or from their bottle comes from.

My view is we need to go back to being caretakers of the earth. We should feel a relationship to the earth and nature. It sustains us and has the power to heal. There are about 80,000 plant species that can cure diseases, not just mask symptoms like synthetics do, but truly heal. Yet only 3 percent of the plant species have been synthesized. It makes you wonder.

Your health and wellness, your well-being are paramount to me. I love ♡🖤🩶 you always and want the best for you.

Good morning ☼! Time is an extraordinary concept. It is a human-made concept. Time, as we know it on earth, passes by steadily, whether we want it to or not. Regardless of what is happening in the world, it does not stop. Instead, it marches on. Today is already history by tomorrow.

This means that everything is fluid. So a tough time will pass, and a really happy time will pass too. It's more about how you prepare and what your mindset is for the good and the bad so that you are always in a stable position and can either rebound and recover in bad times and build in good times. Every bad time is an opportunity to learn from as is every good time. A good habit to form is increasing your recovering time during bad times. You must always choose to grow personally and profession- ally, which will help you as time marches on.

You are a precious soul and may you be blessed always. ♡🖤🩶

Good afternoon ☼! Life is wondrous. It is a miracle that we are born in this time and place.

Think of all the synchronistic things that had to line up over many years for you to be created and born. How many people had to come together in the past so that you could be born as you are. Think of the souls and how your soul came into this physical body.

Nothing is random. Nor are the challenges in this life. They are part of the miraculous process that we and our souls need to go through and experience. We all have a mission.

Even in the darkest times, when it is most uncomfortable, we are in this life at this time for a purpose.

Keep in mind that, as **Robert Allen** said, *"Everything you want is just outside your comfort zone."*

And do not be afraid of what is happening now and what can go wrong. Be positive about what can go right. Go out of your comfort zone to make it right. And know that I am right behind you always. ♡🖤🩶

* * *

Reflection: EMBRACING TIME AND NATURE

As I reflect on time and nature, what stands out is their ability to teach, heal, and ground us. Time, which we can measure yet cannot hold, has shown me that life is not as linear as it seems. The moments of our past shape our present and ripple into our future, for better or for worse. And yet, the most powerful gift we have is the present mo- ment—a chance to pause, breathe, and create something meaningful.

I hope my sons have learned to embrace time with intention and to recognize that it is fleeting but priceless. Whether it's watching a sunrise, spending an afternoon laughing, or walking under the stars in the evening, time spent with those we love or in deep reflection is never wasted.

Nature, too, is a profound teacher. Growing up playing games outdoors with friends, I felt its nurturing embrace. I see now how disconnected we can become living in cities and even in the suburbs due to technology's grip on us and the grind of modern life. That disconnection is why I encourage my sons and myself to seek nature whenever we can, to stand among trees, listen to the rustle of leaves, breathe deeply, and feel the earth's energy beneath our feet.

To my sons, I wish you never forget the joy and peace you found at camp, surrounded by fresh air, towering trees, and endless horizons. Remember that nature can restore you, bring clarity when life feels heavy, and remind you of your place in the grand tapestry of creation. Whether it's a hike through the woods or simply sitting quietly by the water, take the time to reconnect with the world beyond screens and schedules.

My wish is that this reminds you to make time your ally and not your adversary. Live fully in the moments that matter most, and don't let the chaos of life rob you of its beauty. Step outside, look up at the sky, breathe, and reconnect with the natural world that offers us so much wisdom and peace. In time and nature, we find balance.

CHAPTER 9

Belief Positivity

I wanted my kids to believe in themselves and know I believe in them. I also felt unworthy and unloved for the majority of my life. I did not have faith. I was a pleaser so that people would like me and, in turn, provide for me. When this did not happen, I would become very resentful.

I felt my responsibility to my kids was to send a message about belief. Not only to believe in themselves, which is crucial, but they also know that I believe in them and have faith in them. My belief is that my sons are the greatest gift in my life. I also message about G-d because I feel spirituality is vital, and life is more challenging without it. Belief in a higher power is essential because it leads to an understanding that there is something greater than you. I feel that belief provides purpose, direction, and a sense of security to help navigate life with resilience and confidence. Personally, I think that the rising rate of disconnection, anxiety, depression, and addiction among young adults can be attributed to feelings of negativity and a lack of faith, spirituality, and belief in G-d. I combined belief with positivity because I feel they are interlinked. Positivity, like belief, allows people to return quickly from setbacks and challenges.

* * *

Good morning ☼! It was very special being with you all in synagogue. It's been a while since we all were there together. I know it meant a lot to your father having you there. It's always a hard time when it's the anniversary of a parent or a loved one's death. I am glad he had you by his side. We honor those who went before us. We share our love which is what grounds us and keeps us strong. My love ♡🖤💚 for you grounds me as deeply as the roots of a massive tree.

Good afternoon ☼! I hope you're having a beautiful and blessed day. I was at a round table about the recession. There was a great quote by **Jack Welch**:

>   *"Never miss out on an opportunity like a good recession."*

The recession is out of the bag. What do you do?

Follow the masses, listen nonstop to opinions, comments, and online input—fearmongers?

How does the mind react during uncertainty?

Do you panic or make rational decisions?

Do you step back, or do you assess and make choices?

Don't do what everyone does—become short-term focused and lose sight of the bigger picture?

Recession and uncertainty lead to stress. Stress unchecked affects your frontal lobe because stress creates cortisol. Bulletproof your mindset, and don't lose sight of your goals. Life happens for us, not to us. Remember this:

I love ♡🖤💚 you and believe in you!!

Good morning ☼! Glorious day—we are having; quite a few top 10 days this month, and I hope you are taking the time to enjoy them. Whatever time, whether 30 minutes or more—just take that break. I was speaking with someone about my belief that today people are waking up. They are in pursuit of self-awareness. That the messianic time is when the light switches on for all people, they will see the total merging of science and spirituality and the power that created everything. They will understand they can tap into themselves to reach any level.

I love ♡🖤🧡 you beyond science and time. You are part of my soul.

Good afternoon ☼! I am sitting on the roof, enjoying the peace, blue sky, and plants swaying around me. Even with the city noise, it is fine because up here, I just feel removed from it. I'm reading *Hello Soul* by **Alena Chapman**, and she gives a contemporary translation to **Lao Tzu**'s *Tao Te Ching* passage about worthiness.

I want to share this because it is a fundamental insight into worthiness, something many people struggle with—to truly feel worthy.

> *"Because you believe in yourself, you don't try to convince others. Because you are content with yourself, you don't need others' approval. Because you accept yourself, the whole world accepts you. Until you see the worthiness in yourself, your own beauty, you will not understand how to see worthiness in anyone else."*

You are worthy and powerful. You have everything you need inside of you and deserve the best. I love ♡🖤🧡 you across galaxies and dimensions.

Good afternoon ☼! I had a Women Beyond the Table Call. The group is growing monthly, and we even launched a WIX website! The reason I am sharing this is because the Women Beyond the Table started as an idea with no budget, just me and my connections and friends. It teaches us that if we take the first step, the next reveals itself. Be positive and share that. Positivity is contagious; people want to be near that energy and will be on board. G-d and the universe open each door and guide us.

I learned to make a decision quickly, to listen to my intuition, to research, to ask my colleagues and mentors for advice, and to just keep at it.

Even with challenges that come up, and they do, G-d does not want us to fail; it's just an important learning opportunity that will serve you. The future is a mystery, but the present is NOW, and we always have to move forward. Do not ever be the person who lives a mediocre life. Be the boat that leaves the harbor and sets sail, not the flashy yacht that sits in the harbor. Sending you tons of love ♡♥♥ and blessings always.

Good morning ☼! I send you love, positivity, and peace! I really like this quote from **Socrates**:

> *"To move the world, we must first move ourselves."*

I say; start with one step toward something you want.

> *"Don't downgrade your dream just to fit your reality.*
> *Upgrade your conviction to match your destiny."*
> **—Stuart Scott**

I say, think vertically!
Know that I love ♡♥♥, admire, and adore you.

Good morning ☼! I hope the day is starting off really well, and I'm still hoping the "Hi, how are you doing" call from you will come, LOL. I continue to have faith that this will happen—1x weekly! It's okay to aim for a big habit change. One day you may even be calling daily just to say hi. LOL, LOL, I have been checking out **Marcus Aurelius** and like his quotes.

Jon Butcher of Lifebook quotes him often, and while I knew he was a Roman emperor, I did not realize what a prolific philosopher he was.

> *"Our anger and annoyance are more detrimental to us*
> *than the things themselves which anger or annoy us."*

In other words, the stress and negativity that comes from anger seriously affect us mentally, emotionally, and physically. Let go of anger.
I send you positivity, blessings, and immense love ♡♥♥ always.

Good morning ☼! The temperature is expected to hit 72 degrees today. That's the beauty of a March. You never know what you're going to get. That's pretty much life too. You just don't know what is coming, but how you roll with the ups and downs is what makes all the difference. My advice is to be prepared as best you can. Continue to grow and gain as much knowledge as you can, strengthen your mind and your inner self. Make sure your outer environment includes a sound financial plan or emergency fund if things change.

Remember, there are cycles in all things, up and down. But always listen to your heart, or your gut, or your soul. This voice is inner, it's divine, and it knows the score always. It will steer you true.

> *"All the knowledge I possess everyone else can acquire, but my heart (and I would add my gut) is all my own."*
> **—Johann Wolfgang von Goethe**

You are my heart. I love ♡ 🖤 🩶 you.

Good morning ☼! I am sending you love, positivity, and peace! I love you to the moon and back! Everything that you experience and take in is based on how you see it. The pessimist sees difficulty in every opportunity. The optimist sees the opportunity in every difficulty.

It really is vital to shift how you see something, or you will find difficulty everywhere.

Always do what is right no matter how many people choose to do otherwise. Stand for the truth today and always.

I know that you stand for truth, and I love ♡ 🖤 🩶 that about you.

Good morning ☼! I was thinking about the energy people put out and take in. Then, out of nowhere, I saw this very interesting post:

In 1896, **Nikola Tesla** (yes, the car was named after him), a brilliant engineer and inventor, attended a play starring **Sarah Bernhardt**, who was a famous actress of the time. In the audience was a yogi named **Swami Vivekananda**. Sarah arranged a meeting with the Yogi, which Tesla joined. Tesla had already developed and patented the AC motor. The evening meeting turned out to be an interesting conversation for both, as they discussed the notions of prana (vital energy), akasha (the ether or matter), and kalpas (the ideas of the eon [lifetime]), three elementary concepts of Vedantic Doctrine. Tesla became deeply influenced by Vedic cosmology and philosophy. He even started naming a few of his discoveries in Sanskrit after that meeting.

"If you want to find the secrets of the universe, think in terms of energy, frequency, and vibration." —**Nikola Tesla**

Fascinating! Sending you lots of positive energy, vibrations, and frequencies filled with my love ♡♥🖤.

Good morning ☼! From my window, today looks like a lovely fresh day. Clear skies, sun, and fresh air. It's good stuff for the mind, spirit, and body. These are the 3 keys to life. You must balance all 3 and have them in alignment. When you focus on the health of each of these, you will be connected and in flow.

Your energy will be positive and abundant when your mind, body, and soul are in alignment and healthy. The energy you give off is what you attract, so be mindful of how you take care of yourself physically, mentally, and emotionally.

Here are some words of advice from the masters!

"Take care of your body. It's the only place you have to live." —**Jim Rohn**

"You are today where your thoughts have brought you; you will be tomorrow where your thoughts take you." —**James Allen**

Sending you a huge flow of love ♡♥🖤. Your energy nurtures me, and I adore you!

Good morning ☼! My goal in sending you these morning messages is not just to say I love you, although I don't think I can say it to you or think it enough; it is also to send you great energy and positivity.

Energy vibrates constantly; your creative imagination is the receiver, and your subconscious is the sender of energy.

"Energy is the essence of life. Every day you decide how you're going to use it by knowing what you want and what it takes to reach that goal, and by maintaining focus." —**Oprah Winfrey**

I love ♡♥🖤 you in a very high-octane energy way!

Good afternoon ☼! Women Beyond the Table is officially 2 years old. After the call, it was abundantly clear to me that:

> ***"You can have anything you want if you are willing to give up the belief that you can't have it."*** **—Dr. Robert Anthony**

You are amazing, and never let fear of trying, fear of failure, or fear of anything keep you from your dreams. I love ♡🖤🤍 you and believe in you!

Good morning ☼! I hope your day is starting off smoothly! I am reading *The Everyday Hero Manifesto* by **Robin Sharma**, who is a personal hero to me. Robin discusses that the victim-to-hero leap revolves around 2 words: can't and can. Words are the seeds for the harvest you reap. Words are so powerful. They can inspire and free thousands, or if spoken with hate, can influence thousands to do evil.

People who live in mediocrity use victim speak, arguing why they cannot represent heroism in their main areas of life. They use the word CAN'T, which protects them from danger or risk. Life loves those who understand that they possess abilities, capabilities, and the force to shape events on their path—CAN.

The words we use reveal our deepest subconscious beliefs to everyone around us. These beliefs may even come from pure lies someone we trusted early on in life taught us. Try auto-suggestion to reorder your words toward greater positivity and creativity.

For example, "Today I am showing up with excellence," or "Today I have gratitude for every opportunity." If your mind goes someplace during the day to negative self-talk, just do what I do. I say to myself, "We don't think like this anymore," or "Back up, I don't believe this."

So, make the choice and take the leap to bring greater awareness to the language you use and the thoughts you think. With heightened consciousness, you can clean out all the CANNOTS and reprogram with the power of CAN. Reorder your vocabulary, and your confidence, performance, and impact on the world will escalate exponentially. You are the leader and world influencer I see.

I CAN say I love ♡🖤🤍 you and believe in you.

Good morning ☼. I have a tremendous amount of love ♡🖤🩶 for you. I realized something (at 5:30 AM) I thought to share. When the pandemic started, we all felt like we were in captivity—slaves to COVID and the lockdown—it was scary and dismal. We felt powerless.

But somewhere, we released our minds from bondage and the thoughts that enslaved us and held us immobilized. As we tell the story of leaving Egypt and going from slavery to freedom yearly, I really feel it this year. I really feel I left my own Egypt. Moving into the "desert" may be unknown, but it is exhilarating to see opportunities and know G-d is with us.

Good morning ☼! Flying home today. YAY! I send you love and blessings.

I love this quote that really speaks about humility and compassion:

> *"The best index to a person's character is how he treats people who can't do him any good, and how he treats people who can't fight back."* **—Abigail Van Buren**

Treat people well regardless and be kind. I love ♡🖤🩶 that you embody this characteristic; it makes me very proud.

Good morning ☼. Starting this message off with Love first! Sending you all my love to fuel your day. I was thinking about EQ today and happiness.

> *"Some pursue happiness, others create it."* **—Unknown**

Emotions are tools of awareness and consciousness. These are our guidance systems. Happiness is something we decide on ahead of time. Your emotional life is your intuitive direction from G-d. Mastering and maintaining emotional integrity is the key to mastering life. Observing a negative emotion is the key to understanding it. Naming it defines the emotion.

Looking at negative emotion from the outside as an observer helps to frame it and think of the course of action. When your emotions are out of control, such as during anger, the right and left side of the brain stop communicating, and chaos happens.

The emotional state is the frequency we vibrate on. What we vibrate on is what we attract.

You can control the energy you put out. People with high emotional intelligence achieve excellence, and I don't mean material wealth because there are many financially rich people who are miserable, which is the opposite of what a successful life is. Happiness generates a halo effect, and everything is better. Emotions have a major impact on our health.

The best gift I can give you is love ♡🖤🤍 and happiness.

Good morning ☼! Remember, we live in a limitless world. The only limitations we put on ourselves are in our minds, and those limiting beliefs began in the past. Step out of the past and be present. Be present and install positive habits, build your craft, be open, and create a mastermind alliance. Believe in yourself, go deep, be present, and be STILL. Every moment you take care of you, you affect your future. G-d does not consult your past when determining your future!

Look to the stars! My love ♡🖤🤍 for you goes way past the stars.

Good morning ☼! I hope the day has started off smoothly.

It's amazing how things just come when we just relax and breathe. When we are in the flow. It is not about what other people or gurus say we should be doing or what they say is the way, but really it is about what works for you. It comes from knowing yourself. Today I saw this quote and thought yes, the universe does answer us.

Author **Patricia Digh** on the new year:

>*"At the end of each year, I ask myself two questions:*
>
>*1. What do I want to create in this New Year?*
>
>*And, perhaps even more importantly,*
>
>*2. What do I want to let go of?"*

Regarding letting go, remember that families do not let go of each other. I love ♡🖤🤍 you to the moon and back!

Good morning ☼! Another week has gone by. This is life. We get so into our routines that everything becomes automatic, our behavior and actions are almost robotic because we do the same things daily. However, there is the power of serendipity. Serendipity is the occurrence and development by chance in a happy or beneficial way.

You need to create a condition for luck and serendipity to happen and develop the ability to recognize serendipity when it takes place. You have to go to work every day with a tremendous sense of expectation that something good is going to happen. When you have that approach, you allow opportunities to come your way.

I hope you have a wonderful day. I send you oceans of love ♡🖤🩶 and blessings plus serendipity!

Good morning ☼! Another weekend is coming up and here is a great mantra!

We are the Cohens.

We are powerful.

We are capable.

We are limitless.

We are connected.

We have resources at our fingertips!

The best line I heard recently was someone saying "Actually, I can." It's the truth. We can!

I love you ♡🖤🩶 and believe in your abilities.

Good morning ☼! Today is not only Monday, but the lead up to Purim which is an atypical type of holiday because this time, it was a woman who saved our people.

Queen Esther did not use a sword, conspire to murder, act egotistically, lie, or act from hate. What she did was pray, fast, rise to the occasion, use her brain, threw two parties, and saved the day. Women by existence create peace.

The Divine feminine is love, laughter, physical embodiment, compassion, understanding, connection.

When the world recognizes the power of love on earth, there will be all sorts of shifting. All light begins with love ♡🖤🩶. Happy Purim.

Good morning ☼. *You Are the Placebo* by **Dr. Joe Dispenza** is a fascinating book sharing numerous documented cases of people who have reversed serious illness and disease by believing in a placebo. Similarly, people die because of their beliefs in curses and misdiagnosis. There is a tremendous amount of scientific evidence presented in the book, too.

In order to change a belief or perception about yourself and your health and life, you have to decide with such firm intention that the choice carries an amplitude of energy that is greater than the hardwired programs in the brain and the emotional addiction in the body and the body must respond to a new mind.

After all, we are beings of energy. When you change your energy, you change your state of being. You unleash the potential that is unused in every cell.

I love you ♡🖤🤍 with every cell of my being.

Good morning ☼! I found that I was completely zapped of energy this week and in honesty have been for a while. People tell me that they are tired. That talk probably impacts me, too. So, I'm thinking that there is some kind of energy funk that is surrounding us that is low vibration and low frequency. Could be NYC these days or just a temporary shift. So, what can we do? Well, the first thing is we can surround ourselves with people who talk about ideas, growth, vision, positivity, and success. And avoid people who just talk about others and lack vision. Also imagine pulling a white light over yourself to protect yourself against the funk. This is a good idea too!

Love ♡🖤🤍 you. You are my white light and maybe I will recharge if you are at dinner tonight!

Good morning ☼! I hope you had pure fun and enjoyment this weekend. It is important in life to have a great time. The positive emotions of happiness, joy, and vibrancy have an incredible impact on our inner selves which affects our outer selves and the field around us.

Being in a state of joy, of well-being and happiness, is the key to a limitless life.

> *"Your life is a mirror of your mind, your consciousness and who you really are."* —Dr. Joe Dispenza

I know who you are. You are a light. You are extraordinary, and you are limitless. Abundance is in your DNA. You are everything and I love ♡🖤🤍 you with all I am.

Good morning ☼! I hope you had a marvelous weekend. It was a beautiful weekend, so the rainy Monday is ok. Water is life and it can also be death. Ah, the paradox of water.

Everything has a ying and yang component. The key is to find the balance.

Here is a message that came to me from India: Happiness is a delicate balance between "what I want" and "what I have."

It is an inner joy that can be "sought and caught" but can never be "taught and bought." Have a balanced day. Balance is a good thing in my opinion. You keep me balanced, and I love ♡🖤🩶 you and the way you navigate life.

Good morning ☼. **Nelson Mandela** said,

> **"A winner is a dreamer who never gives up."**

I saw this during Episode 5 of the **Transcendence** series.

It's amazing when you think about change, it is due to people who dream of it and had a vision that something can change profoundly or create something that affects the world profoundly.

So basically, it all starts and comes from the mind. Dreamers are not affected by external events; they create from within and believe in their vision. They struggle and keep going; they know the struggle is where the power and knowledge grows from.

I feel you are that dreamer, and I cannot wait to see how you manifest great things to come. I am your biggest cheerleader and love ♡🖤🩶 you forever.

Good afternoon ☼! The mornings are a bit more challenging. It is hard waking up and roaring with energy and purpose. I know that this war our people are experiencing is psychologically exhausting and concerning. But I am committed to messaging you, finding the inspiration, and believing in our greatness to achieve and grow. We are world class. Don't ever think otherwise. You are my world, and I love ♡🖤🩶 and adore you.

Good morning ☼. What is happiness and why do most of our ideas of happiness come from outside? Why are we mostly extrinsic beings? The values and beliefs of others and society become what we believe and strive for. What others are doing and experiencing is how we value and judge ourselves all too often. Take social media. It is the best example of an external existence. People seriously judge themselves on how many likes or followers they have. There is a whole culture focused only on superficial beauty and having it all. Don't get me started on "influencers" who have this fame for what exactly?

Happiness comes from being who you are and not what everyone else tells you to be. Using your gifts to find what lights you up from within. Sometimes we are lucky to find a guide or mentor who can help us to discover and uncover our depths. But really it is up to us to find joy wherever we are ♡🖤🤍.

Novelist and writer **Marguerite Yourcenar** on helping others become who they are and not who we want them to be:

> *"Our great mistake is to try to exact from each person virtues which he does not possess, and to neglect the cultivation of those which he has."*

Reflection:
THE POWER OF BELIEF AND POSITIVITY

As I reflect on belief and positivity, I realize these concepts are foundational; they are the building blocks to a healthy life. For much of my life, I struggled to find this foundation, feeling unworthy and questioning my place in the world. But as I grew, I began to understand that belief begins with a seed, a small acknowledgment of our value that, with care and time, can grow.

Your beliefs can either soar or limit you ultimately. Positivity, like belief, is a compass that helps us navigate life's storms. It is not about ignoring pain or challenges but seeing the light even in the darkest moments. I wanted my sons to understand that positivity is a skill, a mindset that can be nurtured and intertwined with resilience and hope.

Belief and positivity are not just personal; they are spiritual. My faith in G-d has been a source of strength, reminding me that a greater power is guiding us, a love that transcends all understanding. I have shared this faith with my sons because it offers grounding and peace in an uncertain world.

To my sons, my greatest wish is that you always carry belief and positivity with you. Believe in yourselves, even when it feels difficult. Surround yourselves with people who uplift you and never forget that I believe in you with every fiber of my being. Trust in the goodness of life, even when it feels far away. And know that my love and faith will always be with you no matter where you are.

My wish is that this chapter be a gentle nudge toward cultivating belief and positivity in your life and in the lives of those you hold dear. These are not fleeting ideals but powerful forces that can transform our world experience. Believe in your worth. Have faith in something greater. And let positivity light your path.

CHAPTER 10

Leadership Focus

There is a lot of literature about leadership written by the world's top thought leaders gurus, and quite a lot of programs, workshops, seminars, retreats, and coaches are dedicated entirely to teaching leadership and what makes an effective leader.

Some believe leaders are born with charisma, high emotional and positive intelligence, and an instinctive drive to lead. Parents can empower their kids by being consistent and sending clear messages that include the topics listed in the previous nine chapters.

Influential leaders model integrity, accountability, and empathy. Leaders have a clear purpose, discipline, and dedication to successfully navigate challenges and achieve goals. Leaders have an internal standard for making ethical decisions and taking responsibility, which inspires others to collaborate, innovate, and act toward improvement. Great leaders understand the power of positivity and activate positivity in the people around them. They are mindful and appreciative of the people around them and those who support them. Leaders are relationship builders who can get people to buy into a vision. The best leaders constantly learn and grow; they do not rest on their accomplishments but seek to improve and learn more. I coupled leadership with focus because they work together. Without focus, it is difficult to progress and stay committed to personal, professional, or educational goals despite distractions and challenges. Being focused allows people to feel more in control of their actions, leading to a more centered and calmer state of mind, which great leaders have in common.

I noticed at our restaurant that many families and couples were eating dinner and staring at their phones; they were not talking to each other but engaged with their devices. I have been guilty of this, too, or busy with work. Now, later in life, I wish I could go back and reverse it.

It is even more critical to message leadership and focus because many young adults today are increasingly distracted by too many notifications, apps, and multitasking, so they may hesitate to step into leadership roles. Plus, they may also be experiencing fear of failure or fear of judgment because they cannot focus. My message to my kids is to believe in and be true to themselves, be trustworthy, and do the work, and your friends will admire you eventually.

* * *

Good morning ☀! I am thinking about life, the responsibilities of life, the concept of accountability, and the choices we make. I realize that in our immediate family, we tend to inspire and connect well with others, and we have a way of leading more than following. We kind of walk our own path, which is great. But I believe what makes us leaders is that we give those around us assurance and confidence that we not only get things done but that they can get things done too. It is about making people around you better and empowering them, not just directing but impacting positively. With that being said, I love ♡🖤💙 the leaders you are and can't wait to see your next chapters unfold!

Good afternoon ☼! I was watching this digital presentation, and a quote came up that I have heard before and used in my Brand Messaging presentation too. But every time I hear it, the quote resonates because, let's face it, each one of us is our own brand.

> *"Your brand is what other people say about you when you're not in the room."* —**Jeff Bezos**

So, remember to always protect your brand, wherever you show up and in whatever you say and do. When you do it right, you don't really need to market yourself. I think you are the best brand ever created if I do say so myself! Sending you LOVE ♡🖤🤍 and the most high-level blessings ever.

Good afternoon ☼! I hope your day is going smoothly! I am about to head out to a meeting and wanted to send my message of love and inspiration to you. My business coach is a very successful corporate leadership coach these days, and he has a podcast called *The World Class Leaders Show*, where he recently interviewed **Hans-Martin Hellebrand**, CEO of Badenova, on turning leadership upside down. Here is a standout quote from the episode:

> *"Don't complain where you are and don't complain about the circumstances around you: you are the one who needs to make the best out of it, to accept it, embrace it, change it, and react to it. Be active and be in charge of yourself because that is the essence of all development—on a personal level, on a business level, and on a team and organizational level."*

You are a leader and on a lifelong journey. Remember these sound words because they are true for all of us. I love ♡🖤🤍 you!

Good morning, and I love you very much! Leading by example is a powerful tool for positively influencing change in other people. Develop a leadership vocabulary. What you speak is what you focus on, and it grows. Where words go, your energy flows. Our experience is what we attend to, so focus on the best and neglect the rest. Remember:

"What you think, you become. What you feel, you attract.
What you imagine, you create." —Buddha

Sending you love ♡🖤🩶, positivity, and peace.

Good afternoon ☼. Clearly, I messed up my timing today! I am with Aunt Biggie, and we walked 5 miles this morning, followed by me being inside the rest of the day on calls and on my laptop until now. Every time I went to message you, I did the cardinal sin—I got distracted! Here I am sending you messages about focus and resting the brain, and I'm not focusing. The first part of this quote is from **James Allen** and we are not sure who added the rest, but there is much truth in the statement:

> *"Self-control is strength. Calmness is mastery.*
> *You have to get to a point where your mood doesn't shift*
> *based on the insignificant actions of someone else.*
> *Don't allow others to control the direction of your life.*
> *Don't allow emotions to overpower your intelligence."*

It's a work in progress, ignoring triggers and distractions that set us off in another direction and wreak brain havoc where thinking and intelligence stops. A trigger can lead to a complete loss of focus. The goal is to put triggers and distractions in a box on a shelf and make them insignificant. That do not matter. Sending you love ♡🖤🩶 always.

Good morning ☼! How is your Monday going? I hope it's started off bright. I was reading this morning, and a quote popped out to me, and I thought, "Yep, that sums it up!"

> *"The strength of character and emotional intelligence*
> *to face your failures and learn from them are at the core*
> *of success." —Robert Kiyosaki*

I don't just look at strength of character and EQ in terms of business success but in terms of life success. It's about who you are and how you treat others. It's about recognizing we all have a lot to learn in this area. There is a reason in the Torah that humiliating someone is the equivalent of death. You can have an impact either way, in a good way or a bad way.

Choose a good way. The bad way may get results but not without causing the inner destruction of someone else.

May your EQ be strong! Sending you lots of love ♡🖤🤍 and wishes for an extraordinary day!

Good morning ☼. I hope your day is starting off great. Today's topic is the sucker punch. The WTF moment you did not see coming from a friend, colleague, or even family member. Something that emotionally hits you and you replay it in your mind. It's very hard to even process. When it first happens, your mind goes blank, and you can't even answer. You physically need to sit down.

We all experience this; it feels like a betrayal almost. Unfortunately, it's something that happens in life because people are people and often at different stages or places than each other. But I'm here to say it's part of that winding, bumpy, pothole road. And give yourself the moment of hurt, loss, betrayal, and then move on.

Be the leader, learn from it when it comes to trusting yourself and be more cognizant of who you let in, who you delegate to, and who you truly rely on. Remember; don't hand over your power to anyone.

I love ♡🖤🤍 you immensely! Have a great day!

Good morning ☼! I hope your day has started off smoothly, full of light, happiness, and gratitude. Yesterday was a great, interactive, and highly attended Women Beyond the Table call. What made it interactive is that we asked each member to share their answers to the following 3 questions:

1. What were your accomplishments last year?

2. What was the one goal you almost gave up on but are glad you didn't?

3. What are your intentions for this year—what do you want to achieve?

I realized I would love to hear from you, too! Message me! Once you verbalize your intentions out loud to people, you're 85% more likely to achieve them. This stat is supported by science. I believe in you and support your goals! Love ♡🖤🤍 you so much and have a blessed day.

Good morning ☼! I absolutely loved spending the holidays together, and I felt fortuitous you were present at all 4 meals, which truly was a present! I'm proud of the man and human being you are, and I hope you truly know who you are to me and to the world.

Here are some insightful words from the *Tao* about bringing out the best. I have a feeling **Marcus Aurelius** would agree:

> *"The best warrior is not warlike;*
> *the best fighter is not frenzied;*
> *the best conqueror is not quarrelsome;*
> *the best ruler is not unruly.*
> *Bring out the best in yourself, and you will bring out*
> *the best in others."*

You are the best, and you bring out the best in me. I love ♡♥🖤 you!

Good morning ☼! I cannot believe it is the last college graduation weekend! What a milestone as a parent to not only have 3 amazing sons but 3 college graduates! Every milestone has been a privilege and honor to share with you. Thank you for pushing through to continually accomplish and achieve.

> *"When they tell you, 'You can't go on that path, it's beyond*
> *you,' grab that path as your destiny."* —Likkutei Sichot

We were not placed here to do the possible. We are here to achieve the impossible. Be kind, practice the win-win in all your dealings, hold true to your values and ethics, and always be that leader who earns and builds trust, empowers others, and serves. There is no top of the mountain in life but a constant climb.

I love ♡♥🖤 you, and I am one proud mama.

Good morning ☼! I was thinking again about the concept of wasted time. A lot of time wasting is caused by losing focus and getting distracted. According to the author, **Nir Eyal**, it is all about teaching yourself to become in-distractible. Most of the time, when we get distracted, it's the result of internal triggers such as boredom, loneliness, uncertainty, and fatigue. In Nir's words:

*"The reason we get distracted is because we are looking
to escape an uncomfortable emotional sensation."*

You could have an iPhone on your desk or a rock—either way, if you're dreading the task ahead, you'll probably start fiddling with it.

I do see the point because I too can lose myself in doing things that catch my attention that have nothing to do with what I need to do to move myself or a project forward. Even more so, I realize I do allow distractions when I don't want to work on something I am not comfortable with, lack knowledge about, or with something challenging or new.

However, I am going to start with distraction #1, my phone, and lock it away for a few hours daily while working. In the mornings, especially, because this is when productivity tends to be highest. BTW, I still think the phone is more distracting than the rock!

Sending you non-distracted love ♡🖤🤍 and prayers!

Good morning ☀️! Even when there is no sun, you bring the light. Another opportunity for me to tell you how much I love ♡🖤🤍 you and to send blessings for health and happiness, power and strength, peace and safety, abundance, and prosperity! According to the titan of business, **Andrew Carnegie**:

*"Immense power is acquired by assuring yourself in
your secret reveries that you were born to control affairs."*

As your mom, I know this to be true of you. But remember to always take responsibility when you take control. Have a wonderful day!

Good morning ☀️! It's the weekend! Crazy how the weeks go by! Time seems to be speeding up. It's so fleeting. Today's world seems so turbulent and unstable. However, according to **Robin Sharma**, author of *Everyday Hero Manifesto* and many fine leadership books, there is a philosophy to mastering change. Sometimes the foundation we stand on needs to fall so that a stronger foundation can replace it. The birth of something better requires the death of something familiar. To break through to something new requires a breakdown of something old. Our society judges turbulence as something bad, wishing things could just go back to how they were.

This mindset gives the illusion of safety. But remember, the discomfort of growth is always better than the illusion of safety.

Don't stand still; your advancement and optimization as both a leader and human being are built around doing challenging and difficult things.

> *"What is easiest to do is generally what is least valuable to do."* —**Unknown**

Create an inner center of power that is so strong and flexible that nothing can shake it. Build an interior life that stays graceful under pressure regardless of what is happening outside of you. Your strength should not depend on world stability but on your internal stability. Sending you lots of deep blessings and love; my love ♡♥🖤 for you is not based or dependent on anything external!

Good afternoon ☼! My excuse for the afternoon message this time is that we had another Women Beyond the Table call this morning and officially the group is one year in existence. To quote luminary **Elle Woods** of *Legally Blonde*, "We did it!"

I am particularly proud and ready for the new year. It's really all about taking 1 step at a time. That's what I learned. Just do it and the next step reveals itself. Making people feel good, raising frequencies, and positive energy go a long way. I, my co-chair, and our committees put in a lot of time, effort, and work. You have to put the time and work in. There are no guarantees or a time frame when things "will happen or hit." But the beauty is when you love what you do, it's no hardship!

Sending you tons of love ♡♥🖤 all day and night.

Good morning ☼! I hope your day is starting off brightly and smoothly! I still can't quite believe we said hello to spring this week, and next week we are saying bye to the 1st quarter of the new year. It's already another Friday. I was thinking about what would make the world a better place, a place where people put each other before their own selfishness and practice a true win-win philosophy. No power grabs. What kind of world would that be? So, I say to you, be the type of leader who thinks of their people first, and you will impact everyone around you, and they will impact everyone around them, and so on! Sending you pure love ♡♥🖤 always and blessings from above.

Good morning ☼. You are 1 of the 3 best parts of my life! Sending you tons of love ♡🖤🤍, blessings, and respect always. You are a beacon, a light that shines bright. Nothing is impossible for you if you put your mind to it.

> *"When they say it is impossible, they mean for them,*
> *not you." —FabQuote.Co*

Good morning ☼ **light of my life!** I hope your day is starting off the best way, with appreciation and full of promise. Always know you are loved unconditionally and that you are a leader. Believe in yourself, believe in your dreams, and if for some reason you cannot believe in your dreams, then start doubting your doubts. Choose the life you want and go in that direction. Nothing else is acceptable! I love ♡🖤🤍 you and believe in you.

Good morning ☼, **my brilliant, talented leader!** Where did the week go? Time marches on! So, what are you doing with your time? I'm working on self-mastery. Leadership is a hot topic. Most of it defines qualities to lead other people, but I ask, "What about leading yourself? Being in control of yourself, being someone who has good character traits, solid work ethics, and morals. Being someone who practices gratitude and appreciation. Being someone who is an observer and problem solver. Before you can lead anyone, you must lead yourself!

> *"Great leaders encourage leadership development.*
> *By developing themselves." —Marshall Goldsmith*

I love ♡🖤🤍 you to the planet Pluto and back. Blessings!

Good morning ☼! I hope your day has started off smoothly. I look at you and see a good person, a brilliant person, a trustworthy person, a loyal person, an ethical person. I see a leader. As you move through life, things seem like they are getting more complicated. You can make the best moves and make mistakes and bad decisions. We are human and this is part of our experience.

> *"Great leaders don't have regrets about their past; they*
> *look forward. They see their past as a tremendous*

learning experience. In their words, they couldn't be where they are now without the mistakes they've made in the past." —Andrea Petrone

As you move forward, own what you do. Be accountable. Always learn. Know that you are blessed, know we are your cheerleaders, know that you are truly loved ♡🖤🤍 and know for certain that we believe in you.

Good morning ☼! I hope you had a great weekend. I'm happy to be home but also realized that I enjoy Florida. It's easy, feels bountiful and has its own beauty. It's amazing to me that I'm still figuring myself out, thinking about who I am and what works for me. It's a lifelong thing because we grow, evolve, and change along the way.

Great leaders spend a lot of time understanding themselves. What they're good at and what they're passionate about. Their life has been a journey of discoveries, reflections, and self-awareness moments. They used them to get clear about their future. So as the great leader that I know you are, keep this in mind, continue to grow and evolve and have kindness and understanding for yourself.

I love ♡🖤🤍 you.

Good morning ☼! Something that I noticed about myself is that I procrastinate when making a decision especially when it comes to money or confronting something. The bigger picture is not being afraid to make a mistake but learning from mistakes and that failure is not a dirty word but an opportunity to learn. What is life about? I know that life is about learning in all forms across every category in life. It is about making decisions and trying. What is amazing is that the universe stepped in and sent me the following message in a LinkedIn post by **Elle Hill**.

"I'm planning to make mistakes. That's because I'm planning to make decisions. No one is right 100% of the time. So, some of those decisions will be mistakes. And that's OK! I do not choose what I do next based on what I know, beyond a shadow of a doubt, I will do successfully."

The magic comes in acknowledging the mistake, learning from it, and pivoting in what now appears to be the right direction.

So, go out there and make some decisions. Try to get them right. But don't waste too much time trying."

Sending you my love ♡🖤🩶 and blessings for taking chances and being open to learning.

Good morning ☼! Being a king and a leader is not simple. It's a big responsibility and the best seems to put the needs of the people they lead first. They do the right thing and make the egoless choices.

> *"Leadership is about making others better as a result of your presence and making sure that impact lasts in your absence."* —**Sheryl Sandberg**

You are the epitome of this quote.
You make me better and everyone around you.
I love ♡🖤🩶 you!

Good morning ☼. A good friend shared with me that there are five types of people you want to surround yourself with:

The inspired
The passionate
The motivated
The grateful
The open-minded

I realized that I have found this with my network, Women Beyond the Table and my circle. You also provide these elements and more for me too. I hope you always surround yourself with authentic, real people who bring out the best in you and value what is truly important.

I also hope that I am and continue to be a source of love, inspiration, positivity, encouragement, and knowledge to you. Because you are the one I love ♡🖤🩶 the most in the universe.

Good afternoon ☼! I thought to share a few points from yesterday's event led by **Alena Chapman**:

1. We are a soul in a body not a body with a soul. The soul can become part of G-d because G-d is the creator.

2. According to quantum physics (the study of energy and matter), when we are stressed, the soul shrinks and becomes more matter. When not stressed, i.e. in a meditative state or surrounded by nature and grounding elements, the soul is expansive; it is at ease and becomes more spirit. The more expansive you stay the more you are able to move through problems and find the answers.

3. It is belief that changes things not thoughts.

4. We carry our life experiences, thoughts, and trauma in a big bag on our back and pick the reality based on the big bag.

5. Reality is not what we think it is. Power is held by people who know how to manipulate reality.

6. You are in control of what you see because reality alters itself to fit what you see based on the bag on your back.

My advice: Ditch the bag and align with your soul. Open yourself to see the realities out there and choose the reality you want.

My realities always have you in it and my love ♡♥✿ for you is constant in each reality.

Good morning ✿! I hope you are starting the week rested, restored, and in an emotionally better place. I was once a client of and still receive the newsletters of human performance advisor and executive coach **Andrea Petrone**, it definitely struck a chord with me.

"Busyness kills strategic thinking. This is something that entrepreneurs and leaders in general tend to underestimate when adding things to do as if there is limitless capacity to deliver tasks or planning goals in unrealistic timeframes.

What is underestimated is what happens to our strategic thinking when we work in these conditions:

Our cognitive load increases when we're constantly juggling tasks and responding to urgent matters. This means our brain is occupied with managing the immediate workload, leaving less mental capacity for higher-level, strategic thinking.

When we're always rushing from one task to another, we're less likely to allocate the necessary time to analyze, plan, and strategize.

Busy environments can lead to constant interruptions and distractions. These interruptions can disrupt the flow of strategic thinking and prevent deep concentration.

'Busyness' often pushes us into a survival mode where we focus primarily on short-term goals and quick fixes. Strategic thinking requires a broader, long-term perspective that can be difficult to maintain amid constant busyness.

Here's the paradox: When we do more, we expect we can deliver better/stronger performances.

But as a result, we kill our ability to think more strategically, see the bigger picture, and achieve breakthrough performance."

It makes sense. Focus on one goal and still the mind. Let your mind imagine and wander. Don't overload to the point where you stop being brilliant.

I love ♡ ❤ 🖤 your brilliance and hope you protect it.

Good morning ☼. I have been reading *Stolen Focus* by **Johann Hari**.

This book is full of research and information that shows exactly what is happening to our minds and by extension to our culture and the collective due to the endless distractions that big tech, with their algorithms, delivers to us 24 hours a day. This is affecting us in a huge way.

We are losing the ability to focus. We are losing the ability to pay attention.

We are losing the ability to create.

We are losing the ability to think. We are losing the ability to daydream and use our imagination. We are losing the ability to let our minds wander.

We are becoming angry and belligerent as a result of nonstop engagement and notifications.

In addition, humans notice and look at media filled with lies, hate, violence, and propaganda more than they respond to love and positivity. So, guess what the algorithms are sending way more of to your phones? Misinformation and disinformation are repeated nonstop. Everyone believes in fake news especially if it is repeated nonstop. How wonderfully indoctrinating. It is important for you to be aware of this.

The brain needs to rest and repair. With 100 percent of the distractions from our phones by these algorithms it is impossible for our brains to have downtime to repair, to think, to make sense of information. It's especially interesting and revealing that the designers of these algorithms keep their own kids away from it.

Stay tuned for more on this topic. Devices and tech are here to stay. It is part of our lives. I do use tech to send you love ♡❤🖤, knowledge, inspiration, and empowerment. You are my focus.

Good afternoon ☼**.** I have a request!

I would love for you to track how many notifications you get throughout the day. Pings from all SM platforms, apps, ads, reminders, Whats Apps, texts, other messaging, and emails.

Fact: Every time you stop what you are doing to attend to one of the above, your focus drops 20% when you return to what you were doing. Multiply 20 percent by the number of distractions you get hourly. It may explain why your productivity decreases and you may find thinking at times to be more challenging or why you feel burnt out and overwhelmed or why you're angrier.

I don't want these challenges for you. You can check all of the above but leave it all for the end of your day. Respect your time and your ability to create.

I love ♡❤🖤 that brain and mind of yours! Let's protect it!

Good afternoon ☼**.** I hope you are enjoying the cooler air. I like it because it wakes me up, gives me clarity and the ability to refocus.

We are all cognizant that time management is an important topic and a growing concern. I listened to **Abigail Barnes**'s podcast which focuses on how to manage time. It does not attempt to solve the issue but does provide some actionable tips and points for consideration.

It is tough because it is not really our fault for the endless distractions and multitasking (btw multi-tasking was a term coined for computers not humans). We are not lazy or failures for being unable to focus. It is a massive campaign by the many algorithms vying for our attention.

However, whatever you can do to take control, even one small thing will have positive consequences for your brain and life. I hope you get to listen to the episode and give me your feedback. My daily thoughts are of you, ♡🖤🩶 and I'll try not to be so distracted that I miss sending a daily message.

Good morning ☼! I have been on a roll with how to achieve better clarity, focus, and cut down on distractions. It's not easy to do. We are amid a massive tech invasion to know you better and keep you engaged.

Here are two tips from *Atomic Habits* author **James Clear**:

> *"The simplest way to clarify your thinking is to write a full page about whatever you are dealing with and then delete everything except the 1-2 sentences that explain it best."*

> *"The reason people get good ideas in the shower is because it's the only time during the day when most people are away from screens long enough to think clearly. The lesson is not to take more showers, but rather to make more time to think."*

My advice: Take a break, put your phone away, walk away from the laptop / desktop and let your mind wander. Block out the time daily and label it "me time." When it comes to the written word, whatever you write, follow the "sleep on it "mantra. When you go back to it the next day you will be thrilled you didn't send it, post it, or publish it. In addition, you will be able to redefine immediately what it is you are dealing with or need to figure out.

Sending you my love ♡🖤🩶 and blessing. You will always be in my realm of focus, and I will always listen to you. I may not agree, but I will listen.

Good morning ☼! I heard of something that I found interesting but pretty on target to explain what is happening to our minds today. It is called Racing Mind Syndrome. It also fits the distraction, multi-tasking society where we can no longer be singularly focused. This quote (which can be found in several iterations online) really captures Racing Mind Syndrome, also known as anxiety:

> **"I don't have a train of thought. I have seven trains on 4 tracks that narrowly avoid each other when the paths cross and all the conductors are screaming."**

I am trying to reduce the number of trains on my tracks but please know that you are always going to be one of the trains. Love ♡♥🖤 you so much.

* * *

Reflection: LEADERSHIP AND FOCUS

Leadership and focus are not simply qualities to aspire to; they are practices, commitments, and ways of being that shape our lives and those around us. As I reflect on this chapter, I am struck by how essential these qualities are in a world that often pulls us in a thousand directions and tempts us with fleeting distractions and extrinsic values.

Authentic leadership begins with leading oneself. It is about setting a standard of integrity, empathy, and accountability, not for recognition or applause but because it reflects who we are at our core. Leaders inspire others not through words alone but by living in alignment with their values, demonstrating that growth and responsibility are lifelong journeys. They model focus and clarity, showing how staying committed to a purpose can bring calm amidst chaos and direction amidst uncertainty. To my sons, I hope you know that leadership does not require a title or position. It begins with the choices you make every day, how you treat and empower others, how you respond to challenges, and how you pursue your passions with determination and humility. You are already leaders in your own right, inspiring those around you with your kindness, work ethic, and resilience. Focus is the companion to leadership, the ability to direct your energy and attention toward what truly matters. In an age where distractions abound, focus is a superpower. It enables you to tune out the noise and invest your time and effort into the relationships, goals, and passions that bring meaning to your life. Focus builds the skills, confidence, and discipline necessary to lead with intention and purpose. My hope is that this chapter encourages you to step into your leadership. Whether in your family, your community, or your career, remember that your actions have the power to inspire and uplift. Embrace focus as a tool to help you stay centered and authentic to your path, no matter how long it may seem.

The most outstanding leaders are not those who seek to stand above others but those who lift others, showing them their potential and worth. Leadership is not perfection but the courage to try, fail, learn, and grow. And focus is the anchor that keeps you grounded as you navigate life's challenges and opportunities.

As I think about the future, I hope that my sons and all who read these words will take the lessons of leadership and focus to heart. May you lead with compassion, live with purpose, and focus on what truly matters: your values, your dreams, and the people you hold dear.

CHAPTER 11

Life Advice

The first edition of *Text Messages to My Sons* had 10 chapters, with Advice being the last.

As most parents know, kids sometimes respond poorly when we give advice or our opinions, even if they ask for it. Advice is a tricky word in general. It is probably because giving advice depends on the tone in which it is given.

One of the reasons I started messaging my kids about love, gratitude, inspiration, accountability, and sharing of wisdom was because I wanted to change the way I had been messaging them in the past, which were text-filled reminders, commands, or reprimands. Most of the reprimands were how they screwed up and how they could have done it better or had a situation go better if they had listened to me and done it the way I said to.

In my excitement to share wisdom, I realized there is a difference between sharing knowledge and giving advice. So, I did it in a general way; if a message did not fall into one of the categories of Chapters 1–10, I considered it advice and called it life advice since it applies in a general way. I am careful about advising my sons; even when they come to me to discuss something, I find it better to listen, give my point of view if asked, and tell them it is their decision. Even if I disagree, I love them and am there for them. It is not easy, especially when I think they are going down the wrong path, but I also realize that they may have to take that path for a reason. I hope I have helped with my messages in some way so that they have resilience, faith, discipline, focus, belief, and appreciation of life to find their way.

Good morning ☼. Great advice from a smart mom in India. In a nutshell:

> *"Your talent determines what you can do. Your*
> *motivation determines how much you are willing to do.*
> *Your attitude determines how well you do."*

You have talent, motivation and attitude. Here is to making great things happen, to fulfilling your purpose, and to abundance in all areas of life. Amen. ♡♥🖤

Good afternoon ☼. I hope you are having a great start to the week. I am sending you a simple Irish blessing but powerful in the most basic of ways:

> *"May your troubles be less*
> *And your blessings be more*
> *And nothing but happiness*
> *Comes through your door."*

A sentiment that is both simple but effective. How about these simple words:

I love ♡♥🖤 you. It's that simple.

Good morning ☼! I'm very proud to say I'm your mom, and I thank you for that! Food for thought:

> *"Formal education will make you a living; self-education*
> *will make you a fortune."* **—Jim Rohn**

This means exploring, and having experiences, taking chances, and learning from everything. Live your life because every day of life is a teaching and learning moment.

You are world-class—know who you are. Happiness is having all 3 of my sons in the same city as me. I send you total and complete love ♡♥♥. You're amazing, and I adore you!

Good morning ☼. Patience really is a virtue; it's also a great characteristic to have, like discipline. Patient people think more clearly and tend to hear others out before making a decision. Patient people are observers and planners. They may even be kinder. Be patient with people around you and with yourself.

Now in the mom-scape of things, please be patient when I remind you to do stuff. As a caretaker and mom, it may be in my DNA to make sure you get important things taken care of. I also think I am a bit obsessive when it comes to completing tasks, and I realize I need to work on my patience too. I will work on stepping back; I do trust you. Sending you lots of love ♡♥♥ always.

Good morning ☼ **to my sun, my moon, and stars.** I was thinking about true confidence and who is the most powerful in the room. I am going back to this concept because it is that important that you understand it.

So, who is the most powerful person in the room? It is not the loudest person; it is not the best looking; it is not the most arrogant; it is not the richest; it is not the sexiest; it is not even the most intelligent. It is the Observer. The Observer is the person secure enough to stand back and watch and size everyone and everything up around them without emotion. The most powerful person is not the one you may think it is. You are a powerful person, and always remember that. True confidence is not thinking you are better than everyone; it is in not having to compare yourself to anyone at all. Practice observing, and you will go far. You are the best, and I love ♡♥♥ you!

Good morning ☼! It's a beautiful day and a great way to start the weekend. I wanted to share this with you because it is good advice. It made me laugh thinking about how many people I don't really care for, but putting a smile on my face is easier physically than frowning when being in their company. Grandma used to say, "It takes less muscles and effort to smile than to frown."

> *"Don't let fear or insecurity stop you from trying new things. Believe in yourself. Do what you love. And most importantly, be kind to others, even if you don't like them."* —Stacy London

I like you and love ♡🖤🩶 you!

Good morning ☼! I hope you had a nice long weekend! I always find the time frame of November–January 1 to be a fog. It is such a festive time, with lots of decorations and people now going out. The energy is different because people are going out and traveling again. I read this and thought it was good to keep in mind. Words, thoughts, where you show up, where you put yourself, and your energy are everything. Going out and mingling means more thoughts and conversations. Be cognizant of who you surround yourself with and their energy because low energy will affect you.

> *"Once you realize the power of your tongue, you won't say just anything. When you realize the power of your thoughts, you won't entertain just anything. And once you figure out the power of your presence, you won't just be anywhere."* —Unknown

I'll always show up when it comes to you. I love ♡🖤🩶 you!

Good morning ☼. I was thinking a lot about how we react to things. Sometimes it is a particular person, a tone of voice, a comment, a facial reaction, etc. Any of these can produce a trigger that causes us to react in ways we do not like. I realize everything we react to can be traced back to something from the past, something that occurred (often multiple times) during childhood. I was thinking about this because of this quote I read:

> *"Until you make the unconscious conscious, it will direct your life and you will call it fate."* —C.G. Jung

The truth is that beneath anger today lies grief and sadness. Respond to situations; don't react. The reaction leads to choices that have outcomes. This is easier said than done. I am the first to say how I struggle with this. But I know I'm on the right path by trying to learn what triggers my subconscious, acknowledge it, observe it, and move on. Then deal with the trigger productively. This brings peace and, finally, positivity and improved relationships.

You bring me the will to continue to find balance, and I love ♡🖤🤍 you so much for that.

Good morning ☼! It's Wednesday, which was always known as hump day back in the day. This is due to the premise that Wednesday is the middle of the week, and once you get over the "hump," the weekend is here.

I have written to you about the importance of not being triggered externally, whether from circumstances or letting people trigger negative responses and emotions.

I want to share with you regarding how to further remove people who trigger responses from having any impact on your environment, mood, or day. This is from a good friend who is an amazing spiritual advisor and successful entrepreneur:

> *"Take a big cup of water. Put the name of a person who triggers you on a small piece of paper into the water and let it get immersed in the water. Stick the cup in the freezer. The water will then freeze the name of that person. Leave it in the back of the freezer. Every time the person starts to trigger you, just put that frozen block of ice in your mind. You have effectively iced them out. Done!"*

You can use that visualization for any challenge that comes your way or for people who have disturbing energy.

I will never ice you out because I love ♡🖤🤍 you too much!

Good morning ☼! I'm sending you beautiful energy for positivity and abundance. Remember, the most common way that people give up their power is by thinking they don't have any.

Think every day the following:

- I am powerful.

- I am connected.

- I am here.

- I am blessed.

Always remember the only limits out there are the limits in your mind. You are more than you know, and I love ♡🖤🤍 you to the moon and beyond.

Good afternoon ☼! Life is full of decisions and choices. Some decisions and choices we make do work out well, and some don't. Plus, there are degrees of how right or wrong the choice made is. All you can do is be very grateful when you make a good choice and pivot and learn from it when you make a bad one.

> *"Knowledge is making the right choice with all the information. Wisdom is making the right choice without all the information."* —**James Clear**

> *"Always look at the information without bias and listen to your gut, as wisdom comes from a life lived."* —**Tammy Cohen (yes, your mom)**

The best choice I ever made was having you. I love ♡🖤🤍 you always, regardless of your choices.

Good morning ☼! Another Women Beyond the Table Call today. I saw this interesting quote, and being career driven, I thought you would find this interesting:

> *"If you want to be rich, simply spend your life buying assets. If you want to be poor or middle class, spend your life buying liabilities. It's not knowing the difference that causes most of the financial struggle in the real world."* —**Robert Kiyosaki**

It's important to set yourself up by not spending on the fly to just spend but spending your money where there will be a return that is higher in the future.

First, build an emergency fund. Secondly, put money into assets with ROI. Think this way now, while you are young. Anything extra that is not a necessity—cut out. My job is to give you information that I wish I had back in the day!

Love ♡🖤🩶 you!!

Good morning ☼! I hope this beautiful day is starting off smoothly for you. Still reading the philosophy of *The Tao*—I am almost finished with the *Book of the Way* and wanted to share the following from **Tao Te Ching**:

> *"When a person puts on a show trying to appear great,*
> *their mediocrity is soon exposed.*
>
> *The Tao has 3 treasures: Compassion, Economy, and*
> *Humility*
>
> *If you are compassionate, you can be truly courageous.*
> *If you are economical, you can be truly generous. If you*
> *are humble, you can be truly helpful. However, if you*
> *are brave w/o compassion, are generous but lack*
> *economy, and try to help others but lack humility, you*
> *have lost the way."*

Fortune blesses the compassionate. Compassion leads to victory in battle and safety in defensive."

What do you think of that? I have yet to read Marcus Aurelius and see what he would think of compassion leading to victory in battle and safety in defense.

You will never be mediocre, and you have compassion. I love ♡🖤🩶 you!

Good morning ☼! Hope you're staying warm in this sudden NY freezer! Winter is fighting back as Spring is trying to get through. I wanted to share the following from **Robin Sharma**'s *Hero Manifesto* about money & net worth (your income and net worth are so different).

"To realize your life vision, you need to have enough money to create fantastic memories for you and your family and to easily handle your and their needs. You need money to be able to buy the material goods and services that fill your heart and soul, with happiness being a key fundamental. Stress is caused by a lack of economic prosperity. A lot of good can be done by giving back once you have money. One of the biggest mistakes people make in their financial lives—after accumulating too much debt and failing to practice the time-tested rule of living within their means, is to upgrade their lifestyle each time they increase their income. Huge mistake!

If every time you make more money, you increase your expenses, you will never build any net worth and will always be on the hamster wheel. Your annual and monthly inflow matters a lot less than how much you have left to save and invest once expenses and taxes are paid. Don't confuse gross income with net profit EVER!"

I wish someone would have explained this to me when I was younger. I love ♡ ❤ 🤍 you no matter your net worth but be way smarter than me! Sending you blessings for abundance and prosperity always!

Good morning ☼! Just got back from an appointment. There was some confusion regarding the appointment time etc., and the staff was not handling it. So, my first reaction was to be annoyed, and that escalated to frustration with the staff. But some voice said in my head, "Who cares? This is so not a big issue, and it will get figured out." And I calmed down, and guess what? Everything not only got figured out, but I was given VIP treatment. HA! It works.

"Don't sweat the small stuff." —Dr. Richard Carlson

I send you very strong love ♡ ❤ 🤍 and blessings from a very relaxed mind. The point of the story is we can control our reactions.

Good morning ☼! I hope you had a wonderful weekend and an even better start to the day. Starting is the key. The longer we delay starting, the less motivation we have.

There is a huge misconception that you need motivation to get started. That is wrong; you need to start to get motivation. Check this out The Process (**James Clear**—*Atomic Habits*):

1. Decide what you want to achieve.

2. Try different ways of achieving it until you find one that works for you.

3. Do more of what works. Do less of what does not.

4. Don't stop doing it until it stops working.

5. Repeat.

You have always been my motivation to get up and move forward each day. It is part of my love ♡🖤🤍 for you.

Good morning ☼! I have a longer message today since I was very fortunate to receive the perfect advice from a business coach that I had worked with. He coaches executive teams at the corporate level and has worked in 7 countries.

So here are the 6 big lessons from **Andrea Petrone:**

1. Take opportunities when they arise—make it a new habit. Until now, when I see an opportunity with a well-calculated risk, I take it. I don't wait until the opportunity is gone. If you wait to have all facts available to make a decision in the current world, you'll end up regretting it.

2. Follow your own path and not what others want for you—It's easy for others to tell you what to do. But at the end of the day, you are responsible and committed to your own actions.

3. If you follow someone else's advice, that's ok, but it's still your responsibility to deal with the decision.

4. Let other people play safe while you skyrocket your results—Don't copy what other people do just because everyone does

that. Do what is important to you. Don't play safe. Identify good risks to take. Playing safe generates just average results.

5. Embrace diversity without bias and preconception—Don't focus on other people's biases. Form your own opinion. Bias is our worst limitation. Fight or step away when you come across them.

6. Aim for a big stretch to maximize your outcomes—Always look for stretching yourself and look for big stretches. When you play small, your comfort zone doesn't get much bigger. But when you play big, even if you don't achieve it all, you still learn to get more comfortable outside of your current circle.

I think you know all this intuitively, but it is easier said than done, although I think you understand the importance of being on the right track. Knowing you possess the right mindset, determination, motivation, and discipline at your age makes all the difference in living an incredible life. I love ♡🖤🤍 you and love watching you make your moves and do your thing. I bless you and stand behind you always.

Good morning ☼, to the best son there is! Something to keep in mind—our character and emotional headset affect EVERY area of our lives:

> *"Watch your thoughts, for they become words.*
> *Watch your words, for they become actions.*
> *Watch your actions, for they become habits.*
> *Watch your habits, for they become character.*
> *Watch your character, for it becomes your destiny."*
> *—Lao Tzu*

I was so happy to be with you celebrating and listening to great music. May we always be healthy to celebrate, and may we keep celebrating life together. I love ♡🖤🤍 you so much.

Inspiration for the day:

> *"Motivation often comes after starting, not before.*
> *Action produces momentum."* **—James Clear**

Good morning ☼! I hope you enjoyed the weekend! After reading **Robin Sharma** along with other sources, these 3 mantras keep coming up. I decided to create a mantra list with these at the top.

The mantra list is growing and evolving, and you should consider creating one and repeating it to yourself daily. Repetition works!

1. Clean up my thoughts.

2. Elevate my emotions.

3. Choose good words.

Words are interesting because they can elevate or destroy. Emotional abuse, which often is linked to verbal abuse, is insidious and impacts a person's subconscious, affecting a person's psyche deeply. So, remember to watch your words and think before you say something because words have power. My words to you are simple: You are a gift from G-d, and I love ♡🖤🩶 you with every inch of my being.

Good morning ☼! Today the weather looks glorious, and your COVID light mom is pretty much finished with quarantine! Yay. During yesterday's Women Beyond the Table call, one of our members gave a terrific presentation about creating brazen boundaries at work and at home. I think it's a very important topic. Learning how to say no in the right way to things that do not serve you or challenge your ethics and moral fiber is not only crucial but an art. Standing up for yourself and your values does also affect the way people perceive you.

The art is how you say no and what types of alternatives or compromises you can offer so you are providing a solution, but at the same time, not over-explaining yourself for saying no. It's vital to say no to an "ask" that doesn't align with your core, your time, or your needs. Here is a good general tips list for when to say No to an ASK.

Consider a No in these 5 circumstances:

1. When current responsibilities begin to suffer.

2. When it is someone else's work.

3. When there is no exit strategy.

4. When the ask is unreasonable.

5. When it goes against your values.

I do have a hard time saying no to you, though! It's probably because love gets in the way and guilt for saying no, but at the end of the day, it's better to say no in the right way than feel angry, overwhelmed, or frustrated for saying yes. Sending you love ♡🖤🤍 always!

Good morning ☀! You are brilliant and talented—a true light!
A blessing for you: May you always move forwards and not backward.

> *"If you can't fly then run. If you can't run then walk.*
> *If you can't walk then crawl. But whatever you do, you*
> *have to keep moving forward."* **—Dr. Martin Luther King Jr.**

Power words; get there any way you can. Lead the way others will follow! I love ♡🖤🤍 you to the moon and back.

Good morning ☀! Sending you blessings, love, positivity, and peace. I love you very much! I pray every morning and ask G-d to watch over you and bless you and your brothers. I send you these morning messages daily because it is my way of reaching you. Did you know studies say that people, especially Gen Z and millennials, are looking at their phones constantly, continuously, so what better way to reach you than with a text? Remember: You are a worthy, capable, disciplined, and world-class person.
Think of this phrase for the day:

> *"Today I behold the abundance that surrounds me."*
> *—Deepak Chopra*

You are part of the abundance that surrounds me, and I love ♡🖤🤍 and adore you.

Good morning ☀! It's Labor Day, and I cannot believe it. Wasn't it just Memorial Day weekend or July 4th weekend? During the great resignation and slowdown of the economy, rampant inflation, and basically too much of stupid, I saw this quote on the Lifebook platform about finance, which according to LB, is one of the major 12 life categories. This quote is from *Your Money or Your Life* by **Vicki Robin**:

"Winning isn't having the most toys. It's having precisely what you need and nothing in excess and being able to stop playing the game at will. Knowing money is life energy allows you to maximize and optimize your most precious resources: your time, your life."

My input: Cut down on non-necessary expenditures and build an emergency fund. Pay yourself first. Track your spending and live on a budget.

Seriously think about investing in whole life insurance and policies where you can build cash. The premiums are low at your age. Even something like long-term care is not expensive if you start now. Find tax-deferred vehicles. We don't know the future, and I do not believe in worrying about it, but if you take steps now, you can prepare.

I find when you put protections in place, you are signaling to the universe, and guess what? Everything is manageable. It's like when you take the umbrella. It does not rain, but if it does—not a big deal.

To create the energy for and open the channel to abundance, you need to have the right mindset.

BTW, I love ♡♥🩵 you rain or shine. Makes no difference to me!

Good morning ☼! Some days start off great, and some days, not so great. It is easy to believe in yourself on the great days but not so much on the not great days. I am here to remind you that you are a champion.

"To be a great champion you must believe you are the best. If you're not, pretend you are." **—Muhammad Ali**

You are my champion, and I love ♡♥🩵 you unconditionally.

Good morning ☼! I wanted to share a quote that is a bit different than the usual inspiring bits. It's about friendships, the people you surround yourself with. It's very important because we tend to emulate the people, we spend time with.

"With some people you spend an evening: with others you invest it. Be careful where you stop to inquire for directions along the road of life. Wise is the person who fortifies his life with the right friendships." **—Colin Powell**

Those are very wise words. I love ♡🖤🤍 you and am sending you tons of good jujus.

Good morning ☼! In addition to lives, words matter. People need to own their words and actions. It is not okay to be hateful. Social media makes it okay, but it is a disease.

With the Kanye situation and the rise of anti Semitism in the US and globally, I feel like it always goes back to history repeating itself in that humans need to find an excuse to hate. It makes their lives simpler and gives them a false sense of power.

> *"Those who don't study history are doomed to repeat it.*
> *Yet those who do study history are doomed to stand*
> *by helplessly while everyone else repeats it."* **—Tom Toro**

Yes, the biggest tragedy is when people stand by and say nothing or get silenced when standing up.

> *"Every smile, every frown, every syllable, you utter, every*
> *arbitrary choice of word that passes between your lips,*
> *can draw others towards you, or make them want to run*
> *away."* **—Leil Lowndes**

Now when you come from a place of love, your thoughts and words reflect it, and your emotions automatically elevate. If more people came from a place of love, the world would be a much better place. That pretty much sums it up. It is so simple yet so hard for people to find love and kindness in them.

When it comes to you, every thought, emotion, and word is straight-up love. Sending you deep love ♡🖤🤍, peace, and safety always.

Good morning ☼! I was so happy you were able to join me for dinner last night. It is such a treat for me to be with you in person, and I hope you find the experience as wonderful as I do.

> *"Tomorrow is a mystery. Today is a gift. That is why it is*
> *called the present."* **—Eleanor Roosevelt**

Living in the moment, really appreciating, and acknowledging it is the secret sauce to a life well lived. Remember to stop and smell the roses. You are my roses and gift; remember that you are loved ♡🖤🫒 always.

Good morning ☼! Beautiful day—the countdown to Yom Kippur. No matter what, know you are loved ♡🖤🫒 beyond what is rational. The keynote speaker at the conference I attended was **Apolo Ohno**, the most decorated US and perhaps global Winter Olympian on record. He was quite amazing as a speaker. I did not expect that. He is also a very successful entrepreneur. He has a great philosophy and motto, which I want to share with you!

5 Life Directives:

1. Gratitude

2. Giving to yourself

3. Grit

4. Gearing up. Stepping into the unknown—set your parameters and metrics.

5. Go after it. Things don't go to plan or the way you think—you need resilience.

His motto is *"One world, one life, one chance, your choice."* It really boils down to these concepts and what separates an Olympian from everyone else! You're Olympians in the world arena. I am very proud of you and your achievements in life.

Good morning ☼! Words have power. G-d created the universe with words. Growing up, there was a saying, "Sticks and stones may break my bones, but words will never hurt me." I don't really think that's true because words do hurt people.

Remember to speak kindly. I know it is something I need to work on. At times I react versus think, and part of me knows what I am saying is hurtful, while the other part feels good to release and vent. But at the end of the day, it is wrong, and I know this because of the guilt I feel after. Please take a moment to send anyone in your life a loving or kind message.

Speak to people in such a way that if they passed on the very next day, you would be satisfied with the last thing you said to them. **Ben Franklin** installed a 13 virtues system I'll share over time).

He believed is important for lasting success, well-being, and lasting influence. He would focus on 1 virtue for a week and, at 13 weeks, start again. One of those virtues was SILENCE: avoid trivial conversations and using words that are harmful. I am sending you words of deep and abounding love ♡🖤💚 and emotional healing for any words over your life I said in anger and made you feel less than.

"Try saying nothing negative for 24 hours straight and watch your life change." —**Unknown**

Good morning ☼! I hope you're having a good start to the day. I was sitting at our restaurant, Eighteen, with friends who I worked with. We were talking about where we are now and where we were 3, 4, 5, and 6 years ago. The BC (Before COVID) talk! Having those hindsight conversations, you know where you look back at something and think how it should have been done differently, or that if you had thought to do something, then how much better off or ahead you would be now.

Or even the "I'm so glad I didn't say yes to some opportunity because it would have ruined my business." There are a lot of scenarios and different ways things can happen and turn out. I think there are many possibilities that have their own timelines running concurrently. Whichever possibility or opportunity you pick is the timeline you move to. As I was contemplating these abstract thoughts, one of my friends at the table said:

"The best way to predict the future is to create it."
—**Peter Drucker**

It's not really choosing which possibility timeline to be on but creating the possibility timeline you want. Deep Thoughts by Tammy Cohen.

On that note, all timelines in my life have you front and center. I love ♡🖤💚 you!

Good afternoon ☼. I am having a late start! It's always hectic the day after returning from a business trip. I'm sending this message because I could not let the day pass without telling you how much you mean to me. ♡🖤🩶 One thing I have learned as I pivot into a new business with all the things, I need to do to move forward is that it is never too late to start something or try something new. The only regret is not trying.

"In the end, we only regret the chances we didn't take."
—Lewis Carroll

Good morning ☼ to my blessing! You are a superstar and a supernova burning bright. I started focusing on finance; it's one of the 12 life categories of Lifebook. Money is a byproduct of what you do. When you bring value, you make money. It's not the be-all and end-all. Money is something that brings benefits. When you are in the flow, money comes.

The flow state is where our energy is in a good place, where we feel good about ourselves and have decoded some of the screwed-up things we heard growing up that sit in our subconscious.

The following quote put money into perspective for me. Took the desperation right out!

"Money is a terrible master but an excellent servant."
—P.T. Barnum

In other words, don't let money rule you, don't chase it, and don't serve it. Let it flow because of the value you bring to others.

I love ♡🖤🩶 you and the value you have brought to my life.

Good morning ☼ from Dallas! Sending you love, blessings, and prosperity! I'm sitting at breakfast, and **Josh Linkner** is speaking about some big idea:

1. Let's run an experiment—Try new things all the time. Test new ideas; do small tests. Don't go all in; try it and see, then go in. Experiment all the time and test.

2. Break it to change it—Keep bringing new ideas. Don't ever go with "If it ain't broke, don't fix it." The beauty and power of a single idea thought up by a regular person.

3. The Judo Flip—Turn it out. Find an out-of-the-box way to do something that is a tough challenge or obstacle.

4. Use every drop of toothpaste—Take every resource and skill set you have and use it. When resources are constrained, you can figure out new ways and creative ways to do something. Creativity goes up with fewer resources available.

5. Reach for the weird—Go for out-of-the-box weird. Use role-storming instead of brainstorming. If you are thinking of a big idea or taking on a huge challenge or obstacle, have your team role-play and pretend to be someone else, like Steve Jobs. Then you won't be embarrassed to say that crazy weird, out-of-the-box idea.

6. Fall 7 Stand 8—Failures happen along the way. Stand up and keep going. Try F*** Up Fridays. What are the stumbles you make every week in trying to implement new ideas, and what did you learn along the way? How did you revise and figure it out?

7. Start before you're ready and figure it out—You have an idea. Start, don't wait for the right time.

Yes, it's a long text. I love ♡🖤🤍 you and just sending tools for your awesome toolbox.

Good morning ☀! I tend to send deep and thoughtful morning messages, but today I decided to share some humor. During the challenging times, you have to find the humor. Humans will always have difficult cycles to endure, and my advice is to learn to detach from the outcomes. Do your part and let the universe (G-d is in charge) take care of the rest. Build yourself to the point where your happiness and core don't depend on anything in the outside world. Here is the message I saw on a sign today: WINE is now cheaper than GAS. Drink, Don't Drive! I love ♡🖤🤍 you, and that has nothing to do with any cycles!

Good morning ☼! Today is officially the first day of spring. Spring marks beginnings both in nature and for us humans. I have been spending time focusing on my health and looking at my finances.

I have made many mistakes in both worlds, but I feel it is never too late to change course, build better habits, and move forward to find a course that works and I can be consistent with.

Now, one thing I have learned a little on the later side is that there are very solid methods of planning that will bring great benefit to your future at relatively low cost to you now. There are financial practices and habits that you can start and incorporate consistently. Starting at a young age makes all the difference. It is always good to take stock of your finances and create financial goals.

1. Make sure you know where your money is going.

2. Create a budget and revisit it.

3. Calculate your net worth.

4. Check your investments.

5. Set new financial goals.

6. Instill new habits or small changes to reach goals.

7. Contribute money to savings or a fund.

8. Speak with a financial adviser about pension plans, life insurance or a combo of life insurance and long-term care. Life insurance at your age is nominal and you will build quite a bit of cash as it is tax deferred cash that you can use later in life as needed. The rate you lock in now will be lower than any rate later.

9. Start an emergency fund today. It is something that will be very useful down the road.

Learn from me and do better than me. I love ♡🖤🤍 you and want you to protect yourself

Good morning ☼! The art of living is to strive to thrive. And if I can share those tools so that you have advantages and more opportunities, then my life is well lived.

A friend sent this sage advice of **Ghandi** to me today, and since it incorporates a lot of what I have learned and shared overtime I figured I would include it!

> *"Keep your thoughts positive because your thoughts become your words.*
> *Keep your words positive because your words become your behavior.*
> *Keep your behavior positive because your behavior becomes your habits.*
> *Keep your habits positive because your habits become your values.*
> *Keep your values positive because your values become your destiny."*

I love ♡🖤🩶 you more than words can adequately capture and at the end of the day, love is everything.

Good afternoon ☀. Do you know you made my day? Yes, seeing you makes my entire day. Thank you for being patient with me and sorting through the items. Truth is, you never know what meaningful treasures you will find.

This painting job—eight days of emptying rooms, moving furniture, cleaning, putting back and removing garbage was very cathartic. I was really anxious to paint because I knew what was coming as it had been years since we painted. But we did it and your father was helpful too! Now I feel organized and revitalized in my environment which is so important.

But best of all is finding the treasures that hold memories and getting to relive them. This is what life is really about and why we hold onto memories. Some are amazing and some not so amazing. My wish for you is to only have beautiful memories and to live each day so when it becomes a memory it is a good one.

Also take the opportunity, every so often, to go through your things and get rid of stuff that weighs you down, or you don't need. No hanging onto "maybes."

You will always be the best part of every memory I will ever have and that is everything. ♡🖤🩶

Good morning ☼! I thought to share something interesting that someone said to me regarding all the times we let ourselves get aggravated by a situation or someone. Or get really anxious because something wasn't working or over some "failure."

When we become upset, overly worked up, or when we react or respond negatively, our body goes through a series of reactions such as producing cortisol, increased heart beat, and spike adrenaline where the brain goes on alert and your focus narrows to a repetitive thought.

This is all designed for fight or flight, better known as survival mode.

Ancient man had this reaction when his life was threatened; he became stressed and went into the survival mode. When the threat was over, the stress left and the body's output of physical responses went back to normal.

Today, on the other hand, we get stressed day in and day out; by triggers, people, places, situations, life, business so we stay in survival mode where our bodies are constantly producing cortisol and its responses are hyper vigilant.

Back to the wise advice.

A very smart friend asked me, "Whatever is ticking you off and making you upset, agitated and stressed, is this going to kill you or cause your death?" Other words going into stress and survival over a trigger or some comment or situation you must ask yourself, "Is this situation something that I will literally die from? The answer is NO. So, if you are not in danger of death, why react??? Why stress out? Your body's responses are the same whether you are being mowed down by a car or getting upset by something someone says or does, it does not know the difference; the reaction to stress, however, is the same. So why do it to yourself? Save the stress response for life and death situations only. For everything else, become the observer and don't emotionally attach yourself to situations.

Poet **Marianne Moore** offers a simple life strategy:

> *"I've made it a principle not to be over-influenced by minor disappointments."*

I love you ♡♥▨ and bless you with serenity and the ability to let go.

· · ·

Reflection: THE HEART OF ADVICE

Advice is one of the oldest ways we share knowledge, shape decisions, and guide others through life. Giving advice has always felt like a parent's responsibility, yet I approach it carefully. The advice can easily be dismissed, especially if it feels unsolicited or out of touch. But when shared with sincerity, compassion, and the intention to uplift, it can provide clarity and encouragement in moments of uncertainty.

Reflecting on this chapter, I realize how powerful advice can be when it comes from a place of authenticity. Advice is not about having all the answers but creating connections between what we've lived and what others might face. The beauty of advice is that it transcends generations, offering comfort and insight long after it has been given. Advice is not just about passing on knowledge; it is about building relationships. It's a way of showing love and belief in another person's potential. It is not about dictating a path but showing possibilities.

To my sons, I hope you understand that advice is not a burden to carry but a tool to use when needed. You don't have to follow every word of wisdom offered; instead, take what resonates, adapt it to your journey, and leave the rest. Advice should empower you, not constrain you.

As you navigate life, I encourage you to seek advice with humility and share it with grace. When you face decisions, trust that the advice you've received from me, mentors, or friends will help guide you.

My wish is that this chapter inspires you to reflect on the advice you've received and the advice you give. May it remind you that even the most straightforward words of encouragement can spark transformation in those you love. May it guide you to approach both giving and receiving advice with an open heart and a clear mind.

Ultimately, the most potent advice I can offer is this: Be kind to yourself and others, embrace the journey, and trust that you have what it takes to create a life you and your kids are proud of.

The Bridge
We Built

As I close this reflection journey and share my messages, I find myself gazing at the bridge we've built together, my sons—a bridge spanning the vast divide between the fleeting world of devices and the enduring depths of the human heart. Every text message I've sent, every moment of thought poured into a few lines, has been a labor of love, each one deepening the sacred bond we share as a family.

My sons are grown, carving out their own lives as they should. And yet, people often ask me, "Do you still message your sons daily?" My answer is always the same: *Yes, of course I do.* Because it isn't about the act of sending a message; it's about what it represents. I've come to realize that there is always something worth sharing. I open my heart, and the words come.

This daily ritual, small and straightforward as it may seem, has become a lifeline—a source of joy, energy, and connection for all of us. It's a habit that sticks because I've seen the profound, rippling effect of a few thoughtful words. They don't just fill a moment but a space in the soul.

I know that someday, when I've moved on to the beyond, my sons won't dwell on the things I bought or the places we went. What they will miss most are the messages, the words that tie us together across time, distance, and even the mundane moments of life. Because the connection we've nurtured is timeless, screens or signals don't bind it; it's etched into the fabric of who we are.

As you continue on your path, I hope these reflections and messages will inspire you to start your journey of communication and connection. Use the technology at hand not as a distraction but as a bridge—a way to foster intimacy, love, and understanding with those who matter most. Let the messages you send become signposts, guiding your loved ones through moments of uncertainty and reminding them they are never alone.

To my dear sons, I ask this: Carry these lessons forward for yourselves and the countless lives you'll touch. Build bridges where there are divides. Choose connection over convenience. And always remember the extraordinary power of a simple, heartfelt message.

With all my love,
Tammy

This book is designed to empower you to connect with your children in a new way. It is not designed to provide medical or psychological advice. Please see professional help if you need it.

Acknowledgments

I am truly blessed and lucky to have the following people on my team:

Vanessa and Jennifer of Broad Book Group, I knew you would be my publisher the moment we met at the ALA conference. Thank you for your expertise, guidance, direction, knowledge, and editing. Your understanding of why this mission is so important and your love for *Text Messages to My Sons* means the world to me.

Claudine of Claudine Mansour Design, I knew I had to work with you as soon as I saw your covers. Thank you for your artistry and genius in creating a design that beautifully captures the essence of this book and my mission.

Olivia McCoy of 9-5 Books, I am so happy you joined the TMTMS team. Your energy, enthusiasm, and marketing and promotional insights light me up.

Gail Hadani, you are a true artist and an extraordinary photographer. You captured my spirit and essence in every image you shot. Thank you, Eva Notis, makeup and hair artist extraordinaire.

Jane Ubell-Meyer of Bedside Reading, thank you for introducing me to Claudine, for your honest critique, and for encouraging me to take the next step in publishing an expanded edition.

To my besties Sharon and Caryn, thank you for believing in me and for your love, great advice and encouragement every step of the way.

To the Women Beyond the Table Community, my Co-Chair Meg King and compass Lily Iny, thank you for your brilliance, love, non-judgmental feedback, insights, and support. I am deeply grateful to every one of you.

To my friends and family who have stood by me through the best and most challenging times, you have made it possible for me to continue to message and shine.

To my amazing husband and three sons, thank you for walking this journey with me every step of the way, always offering feedback and encouragement and patiently listening to me endlessly. Your love sustains me.

And finally, to my Aunt Joanne, who is like a mom to me and my biggest cheerleader—thank you for your love, belief, and endless support.

With heartfelt gratitude,
Tammy

Works Cited

"056: Hans-Martin Hellebrand CEO of Badenova on Turning Leadership Upside down - The World Class Leaders Show." *iHeart*, www.iheart.com/podcast/269-the-world-class-leaders-sh-91190247/episode/056-hans-martin-hellebrand-ceo-of-badenova-103526932/.

"Andrea Beaman Speaks Out." *Andrea Beaman*, www.andreabeaman.com/speaks-out

Butcher, Jon & Missy. "Lifebook - Design Your Ideal Life." *Mindvalley*, www.mindvalley.com/lifebook.

"Ben Franklin: The Thirteen Necessary Virtues." *Farnam Street*, 4 May 2021, fs.blog/the-thirteen-virtues/.

Chapman, Alena. *Hello, Soul!: Everyday Ways to Begin Awakening Your Spirituality and Live by Your Soul*. Morgan James Publishing, 2021.

Clear, James. *Atomic Habits: An Easy et Proven Way to Build Good Habits et Break Bad Ones: Tiny Changes, Remarkable Results*. Avery, an Imprint of Penguin Random House, 2018.

Covey, Stephen R. *The 7 Habits of Highly Effective People: Powerful Lessons in Personal Change (Anniversary)*. Simon & Schuster, 2013.

Dispenza, Joe. *You are the Placebo: Making Your Mind Matter*. Hay House, 2014.

-----. *Breaking the Habit of Being Yourself: How to Lose Your Mind and Create a New One*. Hay House, 2012.

"Do You Have an ANT Infestation in Your Head?" *Amen Clinics*, www.amenclinics.com/blog/negative-thinking-do-you-have-an-ant-infestation-in-your-head/.

Dominguez, Joseph R., and Vicki Robin. *Your Money or Your Life: 9 Steps to Transforming Your Relationship with Money and Achieving Financial Independence*. Penguin Books, 2018.

fabQuote.Co, fabquote.co/.

"Gratitude Definition & Meaning." *Merriam-Webster*, www.merriam-webster. com/dictionary/gratitude.

Hari, Johann. *Stolen Focus: Why You Can't Pay Attention and How to Think Deeply Again*. Crown, 2022.

Herbert, Frank. *Dune*. Random House USA, 2019.

Hesse, Hermann. *Siddhartha*. Bantam Books, 1995.

Hill, Napoleon. *Think and Grow Rich: Teaching, for the First Time, the Famous Andrew Carnegie Formula for Money-Making, Based upon the Thirteen Proven Steps to Riches*. Sound Wisdom, 2017.

"Home." *Andrea Petrone*, 27 Apr. 2023, www.andreapetrone.com/.

"Home." *Deep Thoughts by Jack Handey*, www.deepthoughtsbyjackhandey.com/.

"Home." *Jay Shetty*, 3 May 2023, jayshetty.me/.

"Home." *Synctuition*, 2 Dec. 2021, synctuition.com/.

Hutchinson, Wendy. *Finding the Path of Me: Awakening to Remembering Who I Am and Why I Am Here*. Alinea Life Coaching, 2021.

Judaism, Torah and Jewish Info - Chabad Lubavitch, www.chabad.org/.

"Keynote Speaker, Author, Entrepreneur." *Josh Linkner*, 2 May 2023, joshlinkner.com/.

Kiyosaki, Robert T. *Rich Dad Poor Dad: What the Rich Teach Their Kids about Money That the Poor and Middle Class Do Not! (Anniversary)*. Plata Publishing, 2022.

Lao-Tzu. *Tao Te Ching: The Book of the Way*. Kyle Books, 2011.

Licata, Matt. *The Path is Everywhere: Uncovering the Jewels Hidden Within You*. Wandering Yogi Press, 2017.

The Megillah (Book of Esther) - Chabad.Org, www.chabad.org/holidays/purim/ article_cdo/aid/1473/jewish/The-Megillah.htm.

Office Masaru Emoto, masaru-emoto.net/en/.

Schreiber, Flora Rheta. *Sybil : The Classic True Story of a Woman Possessed by 16 Separate Personalities*. Henry Regenry Company, 1973.

"Self Coaching Model." *The Life Coach School*, 13 Apr. 2023, thelifecoachschool. com/self-coaching-model-guide/.

"Selfless Definition & Meaning." *Dictionary.Com*, www.dictionary.com/browse/selfless.

Sharma, Robin Shilp. *The Everyday Hero Manifesto*. HarperCollins Publishers Ltd, 2021.

Sun-tzu, et al. *Sun Tzu: The Art of War*. Westview Press, 1994.

Swofford, Oliver. "Good Morning Starshine." *Good Morning Starshine* Crewe Records, 1969.

"Thich Nhat Hanh." *Thich Nhat Hanh Foundation*, thichnhathanhfoundation.org/thich-nhat-hanh.

Tom Toro, tomtoro.com/.

"Two Questions for the New Year." *Patti Digh*, www.pattidigh.com/2022/12/30/two-questions-for-the-new-year-2/.

Walsch, Neale Donald. *Conversations with God*. Hampton Roads Publishing Company, 2020.

Yourcenar, Marguerite. *Memoirs of Hadrian*. Modern Library, 1984.

About the Author

Throughout her career, **Tammy J Cohen** has been a dynamic connector, consistently building bridges between people, ideas, and opportunities. For over 20 years, her company, TC Brand Consulting, has partnered with businesses in the gem and jewelry industry and beyond, helping clients define and articulate their mission, vision, and core values while leveraging her extensive networks to enhance brand credibility.

This natural talent for connecting led Tammy to seek opportunities to help women thrive and achieve exponential growth. She founded *Women Beyond the Table*, a vibrant virtual network and community dedicated to accelerating professional success and personal growth.

Expanding her role as a connector, Tammy launched the *Women Beyond the Table—Beyond the Table Podcast*, using her ability to engage audiences by sharing her guests' powerful stories and insights.

Tammy is also an award-winning author. Her first book, *Text Messages to My Sons: Connecting Deeply in a World of Devices*, received The BookFest award, a CIPA EVVY Award, and was a finalist in the Next Generation Indie Book Awards. Through this work, Tammy discovered her mission: to help parents transform conversations and foster deep connections with their children in a simple yet meaningful way. Her mission has led her to publish this follow-up expanded edition, *Text Messages to My Sons: A Guide to Using Mobile Devices to Communicate and Connect with Your Kids*.

Tammy's expertise extends to the media and public speaking. A frequent podcast guest and featured in various media outlets, she speaks on topics ranging from branding and leadership to parenting and communication.

Tammy lives in Manhattan with her husband and three sons. Together, they own Eighteen Restaurant, a beloved spot on the Upper East Side where Tammy and Sidney connect with guests and friends over delicious meals and warm hospitality.

Learn more about Tammy by visiting **www.tammyjcohen.com**,
follow her on **Instagram @tammyjcohen**,
and connect with her on **Linkedin**.

www.ingramcontent.com/pod-product-compliance
Lightning Source LLC
Jackson TN
JSHW021427040425
81963JS00005B/3

*9 7 8 1 9 6 3 5 4 9 1 8 8 *